THE ART OF
IT MANAGEMENT

IT Strategy Pocket Guide

Compilation of Proven Strategies for Better IT Management

Volume I

By: Rick Spair

INDEX

DESCRIPTION	PAGE
Introduction	4
Alignment Using IT Strategy Maps	5
Bad Communication Can Create Risk	8
Be an Innovator	11
Become a Business Strategist	14
Best Practices – Not to Do's	17
Better IT Using Business Cycles	20
Branding IT	24
Building the Perfect Chargeback Model	27
Business Analyst Basics	31
Chargebacks for IT – Maybe Not?	34
Crafting the Perfect Case Study	39
Projects – Don't Assume Anything	43
Employee Security Awareness	46
Help Desk Image	49
How to Calculate Intangible Assets	52
How to Develop an IT Operations Plan	55
How to Monitor Cash Flow	58
Information Lifecycle Management	61
IT Benchmarking	64
IT Change Management the Negatives	67
IT Governance the Basics	72
IT Value Defined	75
Leader or Manager	79
Lease vs. Buy Determined Using TVM	81
Mergers & Acquisitions	84
Making Sure to Arm the IT Gladiator	87
Maximize Employee Performance with SL	90
Multi Vendor Sourcing	95
Need a Career Boost? Try Financial Techniques	99
No Business Strategy IT Planning	102
Office Politics	104
Penetration Testing	107
Play Nice with Auditors	110
Process Development Needs BPII	112
Professional Services Keys to Success	116
Project Portfolio Optimization	122
Projects with no Tangible Benefits	125

Recommendations to Protect IT Budgets 128
Reduce Outsourcing Risk with Better Contract Verbiage 130
ROI Produces Greater IT Success 133
Return On Time Invested 136
Secrets of IT Productivity 139
SLA's Improve Alignment 143
Strategic Procurement 146
Strong Business Alignment for IT 152
Tactical vs. Strategic 155
To Get a Good Vendor Be a Better Customer 159
Unexpected Benefits of Asset Management 162
Using Correct Metrics for the IT Scorecard 165
26 Ways to Cut IT Cost 170
Implement ITIL 174
Consider CobiT 177
Formal Risk Management 200
Is Constant Help Desk Turnover Good? 206
IT Project Success 210
IT Service Quality Improves with Human Sigma 215
Don't Speak Geek 219
Cloud Computing 222
DISCLAIMER 225

INTRODUCTION

With IT organizations being directed by their executive management to reduce cost while providing more services it is essential that they optimize their performance, and because IT needs to be run like a business within the organization, it's strategy and execution becomes an even greater part of its success or failure.

The information provided in this book is the culmination of over 30 years experience, education, and success developing strategic methodologies and practices that have helped IT organizations change from a static no, to a dynamic go!

Strategies and recommendations in this book have been used successfully by hundreds of IT organizations within every industry.

For strategies that are listed in this book you are considering to implement, it is highly recommended that you research them further utilizing current resources to ensure you have all of the necessary information required for a favorable outcome. This recommendation is solely based on the fact that technology changes on a daily basis.

Alignment Using IT Strategy Maps

In today's organizations, CIOs must focus on IT strategies that are more fully aligned with business strategy. Learn how a strategy map can serve as a visual blueprint for the CIO to align IT functions and services to support the overall strategy of the organization.

What Is a Strategy Map?

Strategy maps, originally created by Harvard Business School researchers Dr. Robert Kaplan and David Norton, the founders of the Balanced Scorecard concept, are a technique for helping an organization clearly define and communicate the essential links among different components of its strategy. It involves shrinking strategic complexity to a set of key drivers that are graphically represented to show how they relate to one another. Strategy maps are created at the enterprise level, as well as at a departmental level. The key concept to remember is that your IT strategy map must align with the corporate strategy map.

Why Create a Strategy Map?

Strategy maps are used by organizations to:

- Align organization leaders around a single interpretation of the strategy.
- Enable leaders to communicate clearly to employees the nature of the organization's business and how the organization intends to outperform competitors and succeed.
- Communicate the strategy to employees on one page and accelerate strategy execution.
- Articulate the critical elements of a company's growth strategy.
- Identify leading indicators of strategic success.
- Validate and test assumptions about what core capabilities drive bottom-line performance.

- Structure a core set of strategic performance metrics.

Strategy Maps and the Balanced Scorecard

The Balanced Scorecard framework suggests that goals and performance metrics should be balanced across four organizational perspectives: learning and growth, internal business process, customer, and financial. These goals and performance metrics can also be embedded in a strategy map's general framework and template, which complement the Balanced Scorecard with a simple, concise visualization of the interrelationships and hypotheses that are the organization's vision and strategy.

Look at the following Balanced Scorecard chart (at HBS Working Knowledge) http://hbswk.hbs.edu/item_popup.jhtml?id=3231 for a graphical explanation of the Balanced Scorecard and strategy map.

Action Plan

Follow these steps to help align IT's goals with corporate strategy.

1. **Month one: choose a value proposition.** Figure out the value proposition that differentiates your organization from others. What characteristics are responsible for your organization's customer attraction and retention? This can be a collective effect of many factors, such as brand, price, product or service, and customer service. Develop strategic objectives in four perspectives: learning and growth, internal business processes, customers, and financial. All of these are outlined in the Balanced Scorecard as well.
2. **Month two: examine internal processes.** Perform the following steps:
   - Evaluate the processes that are in place at your organization. These processes include customer

management, research and development, operational, and regulatory.
- o Determine the software and IT systems that will be most critical to boost the performance of these processes.
- o Gauge the degree to which these processes:
- Corroborate the productivity goals outlined in the financial section of the Balanced Scorecard.
- Deliver the customer value proposition determined in Action Plan Point 1.
- Would benefit from being outsourced, streamlined, or revamped.
3. **Month three: evaluate your systems and IT infrastructure.** Perform the following steps:
- o Ask stakeholders and managers to think about key processes that are most valued by their customers and request that stakeholders report on the status of processes pertinent to their units.
- o Measure the degree to which these processes are met and supported by IT investments to:
- Determine whether existing applications are a strategic fit.
- Discover whether your portfolio is missing strategic applications.
- o Plan to obtain any missing capabilities to support strategic processes, if there are misalignments.

In Summary

Strategy maps describe strategies, they do not create strategies. By utilizing strategy maps, IT executives can make sure that the path they have chosen is well understood and well aligned with their organization's overall strategy.

Bad Communication Can Create Risk

What is said and how it is communicated greatly influences how employees handle enterprise change. Poor change communication can lead to employee resignations, reduced productivity, and the subversion of enterprise efforts. Effectively communicate major corporate change to mitigate these risks.

All in the Delivery

Downsizing, mergers, acquisitions, outsourcing, major technology migrations, and any number of other corporate changes happen all the time. How employees react to change is largely predicated on how the information is delivered. A corporate change that is meant to strengthen an enterprise can actually weaken it if employees feel confused and resentful.

The risk of poor communication includes:

- Increased employee resignations.
- Decreased employee productivity.
- Overt employee subversion.
- Inability to achieve company goals.

Two examples of how an organization can communicate change:

Bad Communication

In order to gain greater funding and grow the business, Company A is in acquisition discussions with a larger competitor. Senior management has decided to keep the discussions under wraps until an agreement is reached. A rumor that the company is a hostile acquisition target has been leaked, however, and there is general panic and confusion within the employee population. Staff fear the worst, and start looking for alternative employment.

Good Communication

Company B is going through lean times and must reduce its workforce by 15%. Further cuts may be needed in the future. Departmental supervisors are asked to explain the situation to their staff. Senior management puts together information packages and presents employee options in a short town-hall type meeting the following week. While employees are worried, their questions are answered quickly, both in group meetings, and on-demand one-on-one discussions.

Recommendations

1. **Share information as soon as possible.** Unlike fine wine, bad news does not improve with age. It is better to be up-front and in control of the change communication than to have it leak out through the rumor mill.
2. **Explain why the change is necessary.** This simple step is often overlooked. Give some background on why change is necessary and what the enterprise hopes to achieve. Managers should also share with employees the options considered and rejected before coming to a final decision. Provide the big picture, outlining the corporate consequences of not changing.
3. **Have a plan, and communicate it often.** Communicate how the enterprise will be dealing with the change, and have several follow-up meetings planned to keep employees in the loop. If the change is big enough, create information packages to hand out to all employees. Anticipate communication scenarios and have action plans for each, ready to execute as necessary.
4. **Don't leak change in small doses.** It may seem like a good idea to dole out small packets of change over a period of time, but it actually ruins employee morale. When organizations heap change after change upon employees, hostility and apathy increase exponentially. People react to corporate change in much the same way they do to death or loss: Denial> Anger> Negotiation> Acceptance. Employees who are

confronted with one change after another never have enough time to work through all four stages.

5. **Tell it like it is.** Often, managers communicate corporate change to employees by accepting the change for them (e.g. "We're really excited about these changes, and we know you will be too!"). This will only cause resentment. Employees don't want to be "sold." They want answers. Be honest about what is happening, and how it will affect employees. If it will mean more work and longer hours, then say so.

6. **Involve supervisors.** Avoid the temptation to have senior management communicate to everyone, which just undermines the authority of supervisors.
   - Involve supervisors in the change planning and allow them to communicate the changes face-to-face with their staff. Employees will feel more comfortable asking questions and digesting the information if it is given in a familiar, less formal setting like their work area.
   - Ensure that employees understand how change will affect them at a departmental, team, and individual level.

7. **Follow through.** Change takes time. Refer back to the change plan often, and reiterate the changes in many forms, including in-person meetings, the corporate intranet, e-mails, memos, corporate news letters, and information packages.
   - Ensure that employees are able to voice their concerns and ask questions in multiple sessions and formats. Make follow-up answers a top priority.
   - Show measurable proof that a change had the desired outcome. This makes change efforts meaningful and tangible, and employees will be more inclined to accept changes in the future.

In Summary

Effective managers know that how they communicate change is as important to the success of the enterprise as making the change in the first place. Avoid the risk of reduced productivity, voluntary terminations, and employee subversion by learning to communicate change effectively.

Be an Innovator

A CEO's level of satisfaction with IT improves as the department moves from day-to-day survival to forward-thinking innovation. Becoming an Innovator increases access to funding and executive support, but it is a high magnitude undertaking not for the faint of heart or the ill prepared.

Correct Categorization

In order to bridge the gap between business and IT, an IT decision maker must accurately communicate the situation of his or her department to business leaders. If business leaders do not have a realistic perception of IT's current condition, they will not understand how the department adds value. This is career limiting for the IT decision maker.

Equally damaging is having an inflated view of the current situation. Pronouncing oneself to be an Innovator instead of a Housekeeper, or a Housekeeper instead of a Survivor, does little to instill business confidence or promote positive change. Rather, it sets false expectations, which ultimately leads to an increased rate of project failure and business disenchantment.

Innovators Benefit from the Upward Spiral

Innovators approach their IT responsibilities from a business-centric perspective. They focus on understanding the needs of the business, performing ROI calculations to support those needs, and dealing more effectively with their end-user communities as well as the executive team. As a result, they benefit from the spiral effect by spiraling upward.

- Innovators create more value for their enterprise.
- They attract more funding and executive support.
- They obtain more and better-skilled staff and funding to continue to drive value.

Conversely, Survivors spiral downward, suffering adverse effects.

- Survivors deliver little or no value to business executives.
- They receive less funding and executive support.
- They are forced to manage with limited resources, resulting in less value delivered.

Housekeepers fall somewhere in between and have the opportunity (or the risk) of engaging the upward or downward spiral.

Create an Upward Spiral

Although 40% of mid-sized enterprises claim to be Innovators, only 10% can truthfully justify the ranking. If you are ready for the challenges associated with being an Innovator, then use the steps below to create an upward spiral.

1. **Communicate IT value in business terms.** An Innovator will not proceed with an IT initiative unless the project delivers value to the business by satisfying at least one of the following three criteria: enables innovative new services, creates competitive advantage, and reduces operating cost. A CIO who cannot articulate value in these terms will not be able to induce an upward spiral.
2. **Create a staged approach to incremental success.** Identify a single innovative project that meets the value criteria and then execute it with excellence. Focus on a project that can be completed and delivered in a maximum of six month. Three months is even better. A project longer than six months minimizes immediate business impact. Most CIOs get one chance to be a star, so make it count.

   - Identify a key business initiative.
   - Create a clear business case for a technology that supports the initiative.

- Perform an ROI calculation to support the business case.
- Provide a clear articulation of the business value.
- Present a project plan with resource allocation and time frames.
- Execute and deliver the project on time and on budget.
- Document the delivery of business value.

3. **Focus on projects that IT can deliver with the same degree of excellence.** Once the project is delivered and the positive business impact communicated, the upward spiral begins. You are an IT star and part of the corporate executive decision making team. The upward spiral continues as the CEO sees IT as business leader rather than a utility service provider.

- To maintain credibility, it is critical not to oversell IT's abilities and under deliver.
- For your next initiative, only commit to a project that IT can deliver with the same degree of excellence.

In Summary

Innovators create more value for the enterprise, enjoy higher levels of executive support, and receive more funding than Housekeepers and Survivors. However, being an Innovator is a high profile job that demands serious commitment. Approach a move towards innovation with proper planning.

Become a Business Strategist

CIOs aren't exempt from the career pressures that face IT professionals in today's environment of outsourcing, streamlining, and economic efficiency. They too must prove their value to corporate executives. Specifically, CIOs need to become more business-minded so that they can express their value-add in a business context.

The Changing Role of the CIO

Many business executives fail to see the unique strategic contributions that CIOs can bring, due in large part to the commoditization of general IT knowledge. As a company's understanding of information technology becomes more and more ubiquitous, the value placed on tactical IT knowledge continues to diminish. Because of this, CIOs may find themselves being pushed out of executive decision-making roles in favor of business savvy CFOs or process oriented COOs (Chief Operating Officers).

Ironically, the opposite should be true. As information technology becomes increasingly pervasive in organizations, so too should IT strategy become more closely integrated with overall business strategy. It is in facilitating this closeness that CIOs must shine. They must communicate the unique value that they can bring to the table as the primary supporters of alignment between business and IT.

Action Plan

The following advice is nothing new. However, recent studies show that CIOs are still struggling when it comes to taking a leadership role, communicating IT value, and initiating strategic initiatives. Failure to excel in these areas now could result in you losing strategic influence within the organization down the road.

Use the following advice to help improve the visibility and elevate the status of the CIO function within your organization.

1. **Track and communicate your achievements.** Use metrics to show that basic operations are under control, but more importantly, demonstrate how IT has created value for the organization. Where possible, report your achievements in terms of financial benefits. For example, tweaking your supply chain management suite might have helped improve inventory turnover and reduced inventory carrying costs. Alternatively, a new CRM system might have improved customer contact and resulted in a certain percent increase in sales.
2. **Get beyond tactical measures of success.** Productivity, delivery times, and cost reduction are important to your job, but they do not sell you as a strategist worthy of leading the development of business strategy. There is a lot of opportunity for you to make inroads here, because most executives will meet you half way - they agree that the IT function is critical; however, many just see it as a way of "making everything work," not as a means of moving the business forward. What business executives want are actionable insights as to how IT can improve processes and create lasting competitive advantage.
3. **Speak the language of business.** You've heard this a million times. But, for the purpose of making inroads with business executives, it's very important that you focus on business-oriented goals in addition to technological ones. Also, remember that business professionals are not as tech savvy as you taking the time to educate business executives on IT matters will increase the likelihood that they will respect and appreciate what you do.
4. **Identify strategic opportunities.** Operational tasks like maintenance and upgrades will not make you a star employee. While these need to be done, they should not be consuming the majority of your time. Where possible, move away from commodity activities to get involved with more high-level strategic initiatives, such as the manipulation and dissemination of information, change management, business process analysis, process innovation, and so on.

5. **Increase your value through relationship building.** This will also help you build trust within the organization. Due largely to the proliferation of Web services, cross-departmental IT initiatives, and the integration of technology across the supply chain, CIOs also must become relationship managers and negotiators, with a focus on connecting with business partners, supplier, and customers.

In Summary

Measuring and communicating IT value is paramount to building a positive image of your department and highlighting the contributions that you make to the organization.

Best Practices – Not to Do's

Committing to continuous improvement efforts within your organization includes seeking out and adopting best practices. Benchmarking against peers is one method used to isolate strengths and weaknesses and using a gold standard is another identified practice. Now that you have a best practice, where do you go from here?

What Is a Best Practice?

A best practice is a process or procedure that consistently produces superior results. Peer-to-peer benchmarking is one method for finding best practices, and can be done with other departments or organizations (inside or outside your particular industry), that have achieved these superior results.

Another method of attaining best practices is from "Gold Standards," which are official documented standards and recommendations from organizations like ISO (International Organization for Standardization), and ITIL (IT Infrastructure Library).

Action Plan

Carefully study the best practices and then apply them to your organization using the following guidelines:

1. **Don't fix something that's not broken.** Weigh the costs of doing nothing versus the cost of implementing the best practice. Just because something is a good idea, doesn't mean it is worth doing in your organization. Will the new practice benefit the company enough to offset the risk of changing the way things are done? Changes to some procedures can cause failure, even if the change is intended to improve performance.

2. **Consider context**. Verify that the best practice has been successful for companies that are very similar to your own. For example, IT helpdesk processes that work for a school, will likely not work in a bank setting. Make sure that you share enough in common with the source of the best practice.
3. **Validate the practice.** Watch for situations where senior management is infatuated with implementing a particular new way of doing something for example, something they might have picked up from a colleague during a late afternoon golf game. Explain to the manager the next steps to take before implementation, and even request access to the source of the information to perform the following:
   o Confirm that all best practices have been researched and proven successful in other organizations using key performance indicators (KPIs).
   o Make sure that the best practice improves a process that is aligned with the strategic objectives of your business.
4. **Look beyond the stories of success.** Obtain concrete evidence before considering adoption of a practice. Here's how:
   o Rule out the possibility that someone, with commercial intentions, is trying to sell you something.
   o Confirm that it will be possible to duplicate the practice, and that it did not result from the work of a lone star performer, which might be impossible to recreate.
   o Ask for results of studies that the company has completed. These studies should consist of using normalized metrics (translated to a common unit basis) to prove a performance improvement and to corroborate the success of the practice.
   o Ask for cost estimates, so you have some idea of the costs that you will be incurring, as well as any associated overruns.
   o Incorporate variability into your assumptions by using ranges that look at best and worst case scenarios.
5. **Dig for failures.** Ask to receive, or research to find, a list containing every firm that has tried to implement the best practice. See exactly who has tried the practice, and then perform some additional research, if needed, to zero in on exact reasons for the success or failure of the

implementations. This might be difficult, as people don't like to talk about failures.

6. **Conduct a pilot study.** Perform a small, but controlled, pilot study or experiment before proceeding with a complete rollout of the best practice. This will save you time and money by determining success or failure before full implementation. Look at the following:

o Compare new metrics to metrics that were measured prior to implementation.

o Confirm whether or not the pilot meets your preset improvement targets and deadlines.

o List the results achieved and how the best practice achieves them?

In Summary

Determining and implementing best practices is critical for any company interested in continuously improving its operations. Recognize what to watch out for so you don't make mistakes associated with best practices.

Better IT Using Business Cycles

Like it or not, the business cycle impacts the IT department. You may not be able to completely control the funding to which IT has access, but understanding where your industry currently is within its business cycle can help you better cope with these fluctuations. Identify and monitor key economic indicators that affect your business to improve IT decision-making.

Business Cycle Basics

The business cycle tracks the economy starting at the trough - the point at which a sustained period of negative economic growth (a recession) ends and positive economic growth begins. The cycle typically consists of a period of moderate growth, followed by strong growth, and then a sharp slowdown into a recessionary period.

Business cycles are nine years long on average. The business cycle for the overall economy has implications for all companies, but every industry is different in how sensitive it is to economic fluctuations and, in many cases, follows a noticeably different cycle than the economy as a whole. Remember that you need to focus on the business cycle for your industry, not the business cycle for IT companies.

How IT Is Affected

In theory, IT spending should be counter-cyclical. Technology investments generally result in automation of processes that can reduce costs and/or improve productivity - key objectives during periods of slow or negative growth. In practice, companies tend to cut budgets across the board when the outlook is poor and are generally averse to undertaking new initiatives until there is a more optimistic view of the future.

Having some sense of the economic future is vital in order to properly time many key IT decisions. Consider the following:

- After several years of strong growth, your company decides to implement an expensive enterprise CRM system. Your company then enters a downturn in its business cycle that results in the project funding being cut off after having invested significant time and money, but before the software has been rolled out to any users.

Generally speaking, the IT department should focus on driving efficiency and cost reductions during economic downturns, and capitalize on strategic uses of IT to grow the business once the economic recovery is in sight.

Predicting the Unpredictable?

There is never certainty when making economic predictions. People often make the mistake of simply assuming the current state of growth or contraction will continue indefinitely, causing them to miss signs of impending turning points. Organizations like the Economic Cycle Research Institute www.businesscycle.com have demonstrated an ability to accurately predict the turning points in the economic cycle using sophisticated quantitative analysis. The secret to their success is choosing the right leading indicators on which to focus.

Action Plan

Don't be scared off by the thought of having to spend days reading economic data and developing complex econometric models. As an IT manager, all you need to do is develop an efficient process to keep informed about the future outlook for your business.

1. **Find out if this information is being collected and analyzed in your company.** Hopefully, this information exists within your company and IT was simply not made aware of it:
   o The sales/marketing departments of many companies devote significant resources to projecting future demand for your products or services.
   o The finance department is another good place to look as they need to have a good understanding of the economic outlook for effective budgeting and forecasting.
   o Your organization may also develop or purchase more general industry and economic outlooks that are provided to senior management or certain employee groups.

It is important that everyone in the organization is working off the same outlook to ensure proper alignment. If you discover that departments are using differing methods to develop their outlooks, make sure this issue is resolved as soon as possible. As crazy as it may seem, many companies do not make any formal efforts to better understand the economic outlook for their industry. If your company fits into this group, consider the following action points:

2. **Make this a company-wide initiative.** Every department can benefit from having a better understanding of the economic outlook, so raise awareness and gather support from other department managers. Appoint a project champion for the idea and then take it to senior management to get their buy-in and approval before beginning.
3. **Identify key economic variables that affect your company.** Most economic forecasting relies on `composite leading indicators' - measures that take into account numerous economic variables that help to predict future economic performance. While these composite

measures are useful for the economy as a whole, most industries are affected more directly by a few key variables. For example:

o Financial institutions are significantly affected by a change in interest rates.

o Demand for `big ticket' items, such as automobiles, is closely tied to consumer confidence levels.

Work with finance and sales/marketing management to determine what indicators have the greatest impact on your company

4. **Identify appropriate sources of economic information.** Once you have identified what economic information you should focus on, seek out regularly updated sources that you can use to keep track of them. You don't need to spend a lot of time on this - just make sure you are aware of the current outlook, and focus on recognizing signals of turning points ahead. Industry and trade publications often report on industry-specific indicators, and provide some market forecasting that can be valuable. The following Web sites are good sources for more general economic data:

o The Conference Board Business Cycle Indicators - www.tcb-indicators.org, US Department of Commerce Bureau of Economic Analysis - www.bea.doc.gov, and The White House Economic Statistics Briefing Room –

www.whitehouse.gov/fsbr/esbr.htm.

In Summary

IT should not be considered an isolated entity within the organization. IT decision making must therefore take into account the economic outlook for the business. Make sure that you are aware of where your company is in the business cycle so that IT can make the greatest impact.

Branding IT

IT managers and CIOs historically have had difficulty measuring and communicating IT value. For these executives, employing a branding strategy could be the answer. Bring a brand perspective to your IT department to help publicize the value created by IT, improve your department's image, ease change management initiatives, manage user expectations, and even secure more funding and support for IT projects.

What Is Branding

The term "brand" is often mistakenly used to describe a company's reputation, mission statement, or core competencies. Rather, your brand is the unique value proposition that you offer to your customers. Used to promote the value generated by your IT functions, an effective branding campaign can help mold users' perceptions of your department, your services, and any major initiatives that you undertake.

Action Plan

Brand building has traditionally been a marketing initiative. However, many of the same concepts that apply when marketing your company's products or services externally also apply when promoting your IT department internally. Use the following branding advice to help communicate your department's value to the rest of the organization:

1. **Start with alignment.** Aligning IT initiatives with strategic business objectives is a precursor to effectively branding your department. If you are not aligned, then no matter how you spin it, business users will be able to see right through your "pretty package."
2. **Assign a brand manager.** This need not be a formal position, but you need a sociable, value-driven individual within your department (this could be you) to monitor the perception of IT within the company and develop strategies for promoting IT value.

3. **Identify your target audiences.** Understanding your audiences, their concerns, and their desires can greatly improve your branding efforts. Take some time to survey users and identify differences between how the enterprise views IT and how IT views itself. What is the perceived value of IT within the organization (i.e. your current brand image)?
4. **Define a value proposition.** Outline the value that you create for the organization, and decide on what perceptions and images you would like to change. If you don't work to build a strong brand (and implement practices that support it), employees within the company may develop their own, less than favorable, views of what IT is all about. In a worst-case scenario, you risk being viewed as a costly commodity or necessary evil instead of as a strategic differentiator.
5. **Measure your successes.** Use IT metrics to track and highlight IT value. Measures of success might include satisfaction surveys, productivity metrics, reduction of downtime, improved help desk efficiency, or quantitative analysis indices, such as ROI, TCO, payback, etc. Track those metrics that help improve your image. For example, if IT is viewed as a cost center, use ROI and Economic Value Added metrics to illustrate how IT has contributed to the bottom line.
6. **Communicate at the executive level.** Actively promote IT successes to business leaders. Use executive committee meetings as a forum for promoting IT value and convey benefits in terms of the achievement of specific business goals. Focus on what is important to executives and put together a presentation that relates to their needs.
7. **Use branding campaigns for major project launches.** Your users are constantly bombarded by vendor campaigns on the Internet and in trade publications. These campaigns often set unrealistic expectations and make idealistic promises. Manage your own expectations and help facilitate change management by building brand management into your own projects. For example, if you are going to be launching a large ERP project, wrap this in a branding and communication campaign. Without getting too

techie, outline the work that IT is doing to help improve processes, and then advertise the benefits to users.

8. **Deliver.** This is key to the ongoing success of your brand image. If you are positioning your department or certain projects in a certain light, then be prepared to deliver on your promises. Failing to do so will undermine your credibility. If you're engaged in activities that are not creating value, be strong enough to admit your faults and identify new ways in which you can advance your company's goals.

9. **Give out free samples.** In the IT world, this means pilot projects that involve end users. In the same way that free samples are used by marketers to woo skeptical customers, pilot projects can be used by IT departments to help communicate the benefits of a new investment and help build a positive image for the project.

10. **Treat your employees well.** IT staff members are your department's ambassadors within the company. If they are dissatisfied, then they are more likely to complain to fellow coworkers and work against the positive image that you are trying to convey. Grumbling employees are also less likely to provide internal users with friendly customer service and helpful support.

In Summary

Being the best at what you do often isn't enough. In many cases, it's also necessary to communicate the value that you create. Market and brand your IT department internally so that others within the organization are aware of the value your team creates.

Building the Perfect Chargeback Model

A longstanding challenge within IT is to help senior leadership understand the value that technology deployment adds to the organization's bottom line.

Implementing an IT chargeback system is one well-known tool for accomplishing this. But the process can be fraught with peril if you aren't careful. Learn the ins and outs of chargeback before you consider it for your own IT department.

The Ins and Outs of Chargeback

In its simplest form, chargeback is a means of capturing and reporting on a company's use of IT resources. By better understanding how IT is used by various business units, IT services can be more precisely deployed to meet changing business needs. The chargeback rate is often expressed as an hourly dollar figure, which is then used to calculate the value of IT resources used by a given business unit.

Implementing a system to track IT resource usage can return significant benefits to IT and the company in general. These benefits include:

- **Better prioritization.** Tracking where your IT resources are being used allows for a more precise picture of where the most critical needs are within your organization.
- **Closer budgetary control.** More regular reporting allows for earlier recognition of problem areas. For example, if a given system is consuming greater-than-expected support costs, a near-term initiative can be launched to fix this drain on resources.
- **Stronger business cases.** Specific expenditure figures form the basis for business cases to address key organizational needs. Without them, it's difficult to make a solid case for anything, let alone a complex IT initiative.

27

- **More effective IT-business partnership.** If your business units understand where the money is going, and why, they are more likely to work closely with IT on projects and day-to-day operations.
- **Reduced IT vulnerability.** Similarly, when businesses appreciate the value IT delivers to their bottom line, they are less likely to revoke IT funding during times of restraint. IT will be seen as a strategic component of the business instead of a simple cost center.

Of course, the chargeback process can backfire if it isn't implemented with care. Here are some of the potential pitfalls:

- **Imprecision due to overly complex implementation.** For chargeback to work, it must be relatively simple for end users to use. If a chargeback system is difficult to use, users will resent it, thus resulting in imprecise or incomplete information. Hard-to-use systems can also waste a huge amount of time, driving costs up even further. User resentment can kill a chargeback implementation before it gets off the ground.
- **Irrelevance of chargeback data.** Many chargeback systems are designed from the top down, with little regard for day-to-day cost-related issues. As a result, the numbers they track may have little to do with actual IT budget performance.

Action Plan

Chargeback isn't for everyone. Even if you decide to move forward with your own implementation, the degree to which you do so can vary tremendously depending on your organization's needs. Take the following steps to determine if chargeback is for you:

1. **Study recent budgetary performance.** IT departments that have difficulty obtaining budgetary approval for new projects and for operations could be candidates for chargeback implementation. Similarly, rampant or imbalanced use (or misuse) of Tier 1 and 2 helpdesk support would also benefit from chargeback.
2. **Build or update your service catalog.** Build a list of services that IT currently provides to the rest of the organization. Include specific systems (i.e. a CRM application for your sales force) as well as shared resources like e-mail.
3. **Decide what your customers value.** Use the catalog as the basis for determining how the business areas value these services. This is as much a communications exercise as it is a research effort.
4. **Build data capture protocols.** Using input from the business, decide how you are going to capture resource usage data on an ongoing basis. It can be as simple as a spreadsheet or as complex as an interactive intranet-based portal for data entry. Be sure to divide your efforts into three distinct categories:
    o   **Managed seat costs.** Determine monthly costs for standardized bundles of workstations, printers, and other common services that are used throughout your organization. Unique bundles can be defined for areas with special systems requirements, like engineering or graphic design.
    o   **Operational costs.** Track the number of hours of work that IT personnel spend on ongoing support work. This can include Tier 1 and 2 helpdesk support personnel.
    o   **Project costs.** Track time allocated to development efforts. These costs would typically be incurred by developers and project managers. In all cases, ensure all efforts are linked to underlying business requirements. If not, recovery will be difficult, if not impossible.
5. **Implement a reporting process.** Determine how the results should be aggregated, who should be receiving the reports, how often, and what actions IT and your business units expect from them. Chargeback can form an increasingly important foundation of your ongoing

budgetary planning process, so make sure reporting supports this process.

In Summary

Chargeback can help IT better understand where its efforts are being expended and in doing so, give IT managers the tools they need to build effective relationships with the business units they serve. But chargeback is not for everyone. Plan a well-balanced implementation to ensure you extract the right amount of information without overloading your staff.

Business Analyst Basics

As alignment with business goals becomes more and more crucial to IT success, a whole new breed of IT professionals emerged. Whether you call them business analysts, systems analysts, business systems analysts, or business process analysts, making effective use of these IT-business "bridge builders" can be challenging. Learn how to capitalize on this valuable resource.

Role of the Business Analyst

It's been felt for some time that traditional developers have not had the communication skills or deep business knowledge needed to elicit user requirements and create systems that meet business needs. Enter the business analyst. A business analyst's job is to bridge the gap between IT development teams and business stakeholders by translating business needs into technical requirements. The fundamental aspects of the job include:

- Identifying, documenting, and validating business requirements.
- Setting the scope of the proposed system.
- Resolving conflict.
- Looking for potential areas of business automation.
- Helping to re-engineer business processes.

Action Plan

Use the following advice to get the most mileage out of your business analysts.

1. **Hire right.** Hiring the right people with the right skills is an essential first step. Two important traits to look for that will make or break a business analyst are:
   o Superior oral and written communication skills—Your business analyst should serve as a communication broker and mentor, with excellent people skills.
   o Flexibility—Business analysts need to work with a wide range of business and technical people.

Nitpicking over points of process will create frustration and impede success.

2. **Train to a repeatable procedure.** To be truly effective, business analysts need a clearly laid out, repeatable, systematic requirements gathering process within which to work, with defined start and finish lines. Don't assume that your new analyst has such a process at the ready that will integrate well with your existing development procedures. You'll need to oversee development of a standard requirements gathering methodology and ensure all business analysts are trained in it.

3. **Insist on facilitation, not gate-keeping.** A business analyst's role as intermediary can inadvertently cut developers and stakeholders off from one another. The more hops a message needs to make in order to get to its ultimate recipient, the greater the chance it will become distorted. The business analyst needs to function more as a facilitator than a barrier between the two groups, which includes finding ways to bring developers and stakeholders together.

4. **Beware of bias and inappropriate influence.** Many business analysts may have a preferred technological solution, or even outdated technical knowledge. Remember that an analyst's job isn't to identify solutions—it is to document needs. Bias on the part of the business analyst may lead him or her to downgrade some requirements and overstate others in order to better fit with a preferred solution. This makes for bad requirements. Monitor your business analysts to ensure objectivity and "agnosticism."

5. **Foster mentoring.** Bringing in a communication and business expert, like a business analyst, could prevent developers from improving their communication skills and knowledge of the business. Instead, have business analysts mentor development staff in business and communication skills to increase team flexibility. Developers are often skeptical of what business analysts have to offer, so give them a chance to prove their value.

6. **Teach stakeholders how to work with the business analyst.** If the role of business analyst is new to your organization, then chances are users are accustomed to going directly to a developer if they have enhancement

recommendations. If the business analyst is to be effective, this will have to stop. Communicate to end users that all enhancement requests must go through the business analyst so he or she can map them to requirements and retain a complete picture of what's being implemented.

In Summary

If you have a business analyst, they are probably the one representative of your department with which business stakeholders have the most contact. Make sure this important staff member is being effective.

Chargebacks for IT – Maybe Not?

Most large organizations and an increasing number of medium-sized enterprises have introduced various methods of assigning IT costs to business activities or business units. However, often the method employed fails to deliver much value. In many cases, the overhead incurred in calculating recharges is a waste of resources. Enterprises should be cautious before adopting a recharge method unless it aligns well with their objectives, and is really worth the effort.

Determine the Objectives

Surveys and research indicate that IT expenses consume an average of 6% of revenues. Business leaders want to know where IT incurs cost within their enterprise. Some want control over where funds are spent. Some enterprises require annual re-justification for IT expenses.

Chargeback processes are implemented in order to help with these issues. These include allocation, chargeback for specific services, and full internal chargeback based on pseudo market prices for all services. These approaches often fail.

Enterprises must establish their objectives for an IT chargeback approach. The following is a list of objectives from the simple to the most complex:

- **Understand overall IT costs–** Management needs to understand the overall nature of IT expenses to provide guidance for the overall budgeting process.
- **Understand costs of specific IT services –** Management needs to understand the investment made in specific IT services, such as application development, help desk, or server management in order to compare costs over time or to benchmarks. In this case,

enterprises are interested in only parts of the overall IT budget.

- **Establish IT pricing for individual business units–** As part of the process of determining total business unit expenses and profitability, management needs to understand the total application and/or IT infrastructure costs for each business unit.
- **Drive demand levels for IT services based on cost-value trade-offs** – Some enterprises enable business units to vary their demand for IT services based on how they perceive value for the service. In most cases, this is limited to items that are truly discretionary (for example, laptops, cellular, and long-distance services). In the extreme case, IT has a price list for a variety of services. Business units have the option to buy these services from external suppliers.

Understanding IT Costs

It is essential that IT describe where it spends its budget. In some cases, there may be concern that IT is overspending on some services or has failed to take advantage of lower cost options. If the enterprise only wishes to understand and report on overall IT costs or the costs of specific services, the enterprise can carry out a one time or periodic financial analysis and report the results. It is generally unnecessary to determine how much each business unit consumes of all resources.

The Simple Allocation Model – Common but Misleading

When enterprises wish to incorporate IT costs in overall budget management, the most commonly adopted recharge method is the cost allocation model. The enterprise allocates overall IT costs to business units based on some common measure of relative business unit size. Examples are allocation by revenue, by number of staff, or by number of personal computers installed.

The approach is attractive to enterprises because it appears to reflect IT costs in business unit budgets, and because it is simple to implement and understand. Business units generally consider it fair. It is often consistent with the methods used to allocated costs of other enterprise shared services such as Human Resources and Finance.

However, if the intended primary objective is to establish the actual cost of IT for individual business units, the approach is flawed. While allocation allows notional IT costs to be included in business unit budgets, the allocation, because it is simplistic, does not reflect the actual relative consumption of IT resources by each business unit.

- Firstly, a single measure chosen for allocation is unlikely to reflect relative consumption of multiple aspects of IT. For example, while an allocation based on number of PCs may be a good basis for sharing help-desk costs, it is likely inappropriate for assigning the costs of servers and storage.
- Secondly, whenever any business unit makes much greater use of IT than other units of a similar size do (which is generally the case), IT cost allocation understates the IT costs of one unit and overstates the other. Any attempt to evaluate relative business unit performance or profitability based on these numbers is inaccurate.

Enterprises can implement a more accurate but more complex version of the allocation model. Instead of a single basis for cost allocation, IT costs are broken up into different categories, with allocation based on different criteria. For example, help-desk costs may be allocated based on number of PCs, and server, storage, and operations costs may be based on the percentage of servers assigned to each business unit.

Simple cost allocation yields inaccurate results. However, a detailed calculation of all of the IT costs incurred by a business unit can be complex. Enterprises should and do track major IT infrastructure expenses, such as servers, data center, storage, network, and personnel at an aggregate level. However, determining what part of each aggregated cost belongs to each business unit requires the development of a complex model and a detailed accounting process. This work is rarely justified.

Running IT as a Business – Only For the Brave

At the most sophisticated level, a few IT organizations operate as a business with price lists for all services, detailed usage tracking and regular monthly billing to business units. The advantage of this approach is that it enables business units to make consumption decisions based on cost-value evaluation. Therefore, business units should incur IT expenditures only if these have value in line with the expense. Additionally, when IT price lists are comparable to services available outside the organization (for example, help desk or managed network services), IT is motivated to keep its costs in line with external prices.

However, this approach has a number of significant challenges that make it impractical for all but a few enterprises:

- **Business unit lock-in.** Most IT consumption is non-discretionary in the mid-term. Business units cannot easily replace legacy systems with alternatives, and base maintenance capability must be in place. The design of the applications makes it very difficult to reduce network, processor, and storage consumption.
- **Complex financial management.** To run IT as a business, IT must incur the overhead of pricing, selling, usage tracking, and billing.
- **Difficulty in matching supply and demand.** IT must align the nature and duration of its agreements with business units with its commitments for equipment depreciation, labor, and service contracts. Unlike an independent business, IT cannot negotiate a lower price with

some business units to sell excess labor or infrastructure capacity. In addition, IT typically cannot sell outside the enterprise.

- **Funding.** If the businesses can vary their individual and collective consumption, IT will experience revenue and cost imbalances, at least in the short term. IT will need a source of investment funds to ensure working capital. In addition, IT will require capital funds to provide infrastructure capability (servers, storage, Local Area Networks, and telephone systems).

Recommendations

IT may be able to provide sufficient financial transparency to their enterprise without creating a recharge mechanism.

1. **Start by reporting IT costs.** Most enterprises can make intelligent IT budget decisions based on overall or focused cost analysis. Recharge is not necessary.
2. **Allocate IT costs only if cost allocation is a broad enterprise practice.** Allocation of IT costs is appropriate as part of an enterprise-wide practice. It is not a good basis for assessing the value-cost relationship of IT.
3. **Avoid detailed IT chargeback.** Implement detailed calculation and chargeback of costs only if business units are empowered to make significant IT budgeting choices. Otherwise, detailed analysis of costs by individual business has little effect on actual IT expenditures.

Summary

A number of methods have evolved for charging back IT costs to business units. Some of these approaches, however, misrepresent the actual IT cost incurred by business units. Establish clear objectives for a chargeback process and adopt a recharge approach only if it is appropriate to these objectives.

Crafting the Perfect Case Study

Case studies are also referred to as success stories, customer profiles, or case histories. Use a case study to demonstrate how a specific situation or problem was initially identified, alternative solutions researched, and a final solution selected to resolve the problem.

Why Create Case Studies?

- **As an effective knowledge management tool.** Generating case studies is one way to harness your knowledge-based assets. For example, use case studies to learn how you handled a past system integration, or to avoid problems you faced implementing a specific technology.
- **As a powerful tool to market your IT products and services.** Case studies are a very influential and powerful marketing tool. These studies can focus on your organization's or your customers' successes with your IT products or services. Use these types of case studies to show the value of your IT department to the rest of your organization.

Action Plan

1. **Define the type of case study.** Before you begin, you need to decide which kind of case study you are going to write and who your audience is going to be. A case study that is to be used for internal knowledge management will be written very differently than one that is to be used as a marketing tool.
2. **Be consistent when writing case studies.** Case studies are best written after every significant project effort that goes beyond day to day business execution especially if they are written for internal knowledge management. More often than not, most companies write a case study only when they want to flaunt their

successes; as a result, they miss-out on some valuable future reference and learning material. A consistent structure and layout to your case studies makes them easier to read and write.

3. **Follow some basic rules.** Here are some best practices for writing case studies:
   o Use the words "case study" in your title.
   o Always write about an issue that has significant impact for the reader and keep your audience in mind.
   o Support your study with figures, tables, and statistics where appropriate. Make sure key stats are highlighted.
   o Don't overload the case study with too much technical jargon and too many statistics.
   o Get names, titles, and quotes from every person who is interviewed.
   o Mention both the targeted and achieved ROI (Return on Investment) when appropriate.

4. **Write an informative and effective introduction.** Before writing the body of the case study, whether it is your organization or an organization that uses your products/services, make sure that you include the following in your introduction:
   o Include the business the organization is in, the value the business provides to its customers, and the most important issue(s) facing the organization.
   o Provide some background information on the business climate at the time (e.g. system integration as a result of a merger), and the characteristics of the industry the organization is in.
   o Include the background of the organization (age, size, growth, market share, business model).

5. **Refrain from writing a novel.** Case studies do not have to be long and complicated, and should follow a consistent format. This will make researching easier if they are being used for internal knowledge management purposes. Make sure your case studies include all the pertinent information, but keep them as short as possible, and include one graphic per page at most. The "substance" of your case study should include the following components:

- o **The problem, challenge, or issue.** Gather the issues relevant to the present problem/situation. Include any formal analysis done at the beginning of the project as a supplement to your case study. Understand the role of each person involved and how it relates to the problems or issues at hand. Distinguish symptoms of the problem from the actual problem(s) itself. The reader wants candor and to see the point of pain.
- o **Any alternatives considered.** Mention several alternative approaches or solutions considered in solving the problem, and why they didn't or wouldn't work out.
- o **Adopted solution or approach.** Include the reasons and support for the final recommendations and any amendments if contingencies arose.
- o **Final outcome, results of current situation, and lessons learned.** Without some results and information regarding your current state, the case study will not be as powerful as it could be.
6. **Include any roadblocks or mishaps.** Ensure that you mention specific challenges that arose during the project. Include how you dealt with or worked-around the situation and what the outcome was. Don't be afraid to mention failures. If you don't include this information, you will be doing yourself a great injustice. Some possible challenges could include:
   - o Problems with the vendor not delivering as promised.
   - o Project costs went out of control.
   - o Loss of key members of the project team.
   - o Change in the organizational structure or internal politics.
7. **Highlight benefits of IT products and services.** If you are writing a case study to market your IT products and services, whether internally or externally, adhere to the following pieces of advice:
   - o Include a benefit in the title of your case study (e.g. Case Study: How <Your Product/Service> Improved Sales by 200 Percent).
   - o Explain how the implementation of your products/services occurred. What were the issues?

How long before the solution was up and running? How did you go "above and beyond" to satisfy your customer?

o Explain how your products or services can solve the organization's problem in measurable and quantifiable terms, and how the organization found out about your products/services.

o Explain how the investment in your product/service paid for itself by increasing productivity or decreasing errors.

o Show how your products/services have solved the organization's problem. Show revenue gains, savings, and sales growth - use hard numbers.

o Include a customer quotation or testimonial.

o Demonstrate how your product/service improved operations, for example:
  ▪ Share how it integrates with critical applications.
  ▪ Explain how it fits into the organization's business processes.
  ▪ Highlight impacts on employees and benefits to customers.

o Use your case studies in one or more of the following manners:
  ▪ In a press release.
  ▪ In a newsletter.
  ▪ Mail it to prospective customers.
  ▪ Give it to sales as a speaking topic.
  ▪ For testimonials.
  ▪ As a trade show handout.
  ▪ Post it on your Web site.

In Summary

Whatever your reasoning for choosing to write a case study, ensure that you follow these best practices to give it the impact it needs to be effective and to give the intended readers a valuable take away.

Projects – Don't Assume Anything

Assumptions are events and circumstances taken as true without proof. They need to occur for the project to be successful, and are outside the total control of the project team. Create a plan to uncover and manage your project assumptions to ensure they don't sneak up on you and attack your otherwise successful project.

The Danger of Assumptions

What turns assumptions into project-slayers is not communicating and announcing the basis of an assumption so that its authenticity can be verified. This is why it is important for stakeholders to understand and agree on assumptions at the project onset - before they impact the project.

Two common types of assumptions that are especially associated with software projects:

- **False Assumptions:** These are hidden assumptions where everyone assumes something to be true. For example, the whole project team is convinced that customers will really like their product and will be willing to pay lots of money for it.
- **Ambiguous Assumptions:** These occur when different stakeholders make different assumptions about the same important issue. For example, a marketing stakeholder assumes that a product is finished when really the development manager views it as simply a prototype.

Action Plan

To uncover, control, and manage these assumptions, you must create a plan to address them from the project onset. Perform the following steps to set up your plan:

1. **Begin with some documentation.** Create a spreadsheet that lists all of the major stakeholders involved with the project. For each stakeholder, document every single assumption that each of these critical players might be making. Assumptions can relate to technology, expectations, resources, schedules, scope, and so on.
2. **Request a meeting.** Send out a meeting request to all project stakeholders. Confirm whether the assumptions that you've documented are true and shared amongst all stakeholders. Make sure that you have sufficient representation from different departments, such as legal, quality assurance (QA), marketing, support, and development. Gather all of the stakeholders in the same room to discuss their assumptions together - after all, they will be the ones to face the consequences of their false and ambiguous assumptions.
3. **Dig for assumptions.** Turn up as many assumptions as you possibly can during these meetings. Stakeholders have likely made assumptions that they aren't even aware of, consider asking the following types of questions:
    o What problems are we really trying to solve?
    o What problems might a highly successful solution create?
4. **Prepare an early project risk analysis.** Use assumptions and constraints as a starting point to help you with initial risk analysis. For example, if your project depends on the work of others, do they understand your dependency and agree to the handoff dates (which are dates that constrain your project)? This will help you build mitigation strategies for the major assumptions that, if eventually proven incorrect, could seriously impact the project. Also, it allows for the assessment of constraints and the opportunity to manage them to prevent a negative impact on the project. Keep the following in mind:
    o Identify the unknowns in a project and make assumptions about them. Many aspects of a project are still unknown

or undetermined at the beginning phases of the project.
- o Describe project assumptions and constraints clearly and briefly based on your current knowledge. Give extra consideration to resources, timing, and cost surrounding the project where assumptions typically reside.
- o Include any major dependencies that the project relies on as either constraints or assumptions.
- o Alter the estimates and activities in the project plan if constraints and assumptions change at a later date or are nullified.
5. **Think about the future.** Once all assumptions have been identified and validated, make sure you keep your assumption and risk analysis documents updated throughout the project lifecycle. To ensure this happens, do the following:
   - o Frequently revisit the assumptions documentation during project meetings with stakeholders to ensure that there aren't any new or changed assumptions. Expect to encounter more assumptions that will need to be discussed and resolved. Also, be prepared to discover that some assumptions initially thought to be true will turn out to be false.
   - o Appoint a person/people to be responsible for updating and maintaining the assumption and risk analysis documentation.

In Summary

Uncovering and managing assumptions is not difficult, but it can take some organizing. Don't just assume that all assumptions are correct; instead, have a plan in place to identify and manage.

Employee Security Awareness

While perimeter defenses are critical to preserving the integrity of your systems and data from outside attack, equal attention must be placed on security threats posed by internal users. In conjunction with the usual policies and non-disclosure forms, control the human risk by creating a program to raise security awareness in all employees.

Playing Big Brother

No one wants to play the bad guy by monitoring every single action that a user makes. However, the unfortunate reality is that a good portion of security breaches are caused by staff members, whether inadvertently or intentionally. Incidents of both kinds come in a variety of forms:

- Theft of credit card or other financial information by unethical employees.
- Opening infected e-mail attachments from unknown or untrusted senders.
- Forgetting to log off workstations at the end of the day.
- Disclosing passwords to coworkers, family, or friends.
- Installing unauthorized software on workstation PCs.

Act First, Think Later

It's one thing to foster a corporate culture that embraces security as a core value, but it's quite another to do so at the sacrifice of actual security technology investments. Gartner recommends that before companies even start thinking about implementing a security awareness program, they should:

- Solidify and strengthen all enterprise security systems and technologies.

- Establish formal practices and support for workers using these systems.
- Invest in security awareness only when the two previous steps are complete.

Action Plan

A successful security awareness program is one that compels all employees to take an equal share of the responsibility for the security of company assets. Bear in mind, however, that awareness alone can never replace comprehensive security policies.

1. **Define your expectations for the users.** Raising awareness ultimately means changing people's behavior. In addition to your existing non-disclosure and technology acceptable use policies, speak with HR to make employee information security responsibilities a condition of employment (strictly on a per case basis, of course). Also:
   o Give precise descriptions of what actually constitutes a security incident.
   o Establish concise instructions for reporting security breaches, events, or incidents.
   o Conduct basic security awareness "lunch and learn" sessions for staff members.
   o Be sure to clearly post all security-related documents on the company's intranet.
2. **Make employees the centerpiece of attention.** Stress partnerships and people, not technology and policing. Empower them by stating their critical role in information security. For example, avoid statements that say "Do this," or "Don't do that." Instead, use proactive, collaborative wording like "Your role is [...]," or "You can make a difference by [...]." Try to use disciplinary action as a last resort only.
3. **Measure the effectiveness of the program.** Periodic security quizzes or tests are a good way to promote and

measure the program's success among the employee base. Another method is to put a counter on the number of hits on the security documents section of the intranet. Where possible, employ power users within various departments to help you spread the word and make progress checks.

4. **Communicate successes.** Keep the lines of communication open with employees. Send out updates on existing and future security initiatives, as well as the background or rationale behind such decisions. If possible, set up a graphic security "barometer" on the corporate intranet to display the organization's current security status.

5. **Keep the program flexible.** What is considered a security best practice today might be obsolete tomorrow. Allow for some elasticity in your program, taking into account such factors as: changing business models and/or objectives; the introduction of new technologies; emerging security threats and/or new viruses; and growth of the network and the user base (i.e. resulting in a greater number of points of vulnerability).

6. **Expect realistic results, not miracles.** Malicious insiders in particular will remain difficult to stop by implementing a security awareness program, especially if they are determined to hack and burn. It's kind of like the federal government enacting a law that restricts the number of bullets allowed in a gun, and then expecting bank robbers to obey it. Still, simply conveying the repercussions of security breaches to employees will go a long way towards preventing them.

In Summary

Security is a challenge, made all the more difficult by human error. Institute an awareness program to strengthen the security chain and emphasize user responsibility.

Help Desk Image

Your internal IT help desk exists to maximize worker productivity and ensure the continuity of workflow. Yet more often than not, employees disregard the help desk in favor of help from co-workers, power users, or Web resources - this is not a good thing. Brand your help desk and market its presence to bring users back into the fold.

Business Benefits

The payback from a help desk is clear: it gets the user up, running, and back to work. While the business benefits of having a help desk are obvious, pushing staff to use it more frequently has its own advantages. Increased help desk usage will:

- Prevent non-standard or questionable fix processes from entering the workplace.
- Maximize current investments in help desk technology and IT staff.
- Optimize productivity by directing all support through the appropriate channel.
- Reduce hidden costs caused by problems not acted upon.
- Establish realistic expectations for the fulfillment of service level agreements.
- Improve morale of, and communication between, end users and help desk staff.

Action Plan

Help desks have traditionally been a thankless, lackluster department that most IT staff wouldn't touch with a ten-foot pole. Use these steps to build and promote the help desk's image across the organization.

1. **Lay the foundation for a marketing strategy.** Whatever you promise or refer to in the campaign, you and the help desk must be prepared to deliver on it, or

else your plans will belly flop. Remember, your goal is to increase help desk usage by end users - failure to satisfy will only drive them further away. In order to make sure this doesn't happen, you will have to:

o   Redesign or massage existing help desk services so that they are in tune with end user requirements.

o   Obtain senior management support for the marketing campaign. Executive team members must view the help desk as a strategic tool within the company.

2. **Staff the help desk with the right people.** Help desks are about eliciting information to get the user operational again. In this sense, help desk staff are a cross between educator and mechanic. Your staff, therefore, must be technically proficient while exhibiting soft skills such as communication, coaching, and diplomacy. Patience is also critical when dealing with less tech-savvy individuals, and puts a good public face on the help desk.

o   Help desk workers who are deliberately and overly technical simply to show off are counterproductive to the help desk's mission.

o   Find help desk people who always have one eye on prevention, rather than just fixing problems all the time - they will be crucial in developing new processes.

3. **Create a mission or vision statement.** A help desk mission statement is meant to convey the purpose, services, and values of the department. It should act as the guiding principle, the "reason for being" for the help desk team, and should support the overriding mission of the organization.

4. **Disseminate an information package about the help desk.** In addition to the mission statement, include a copy of the help desk's org chart, location and hours of operation, a list of provided services, help desk policies and procedures, and service level agreements. Again, be realistic in what you promise, or risk getting a flood of requests that the help desk isn't prepared for.

o   Post this package on the corporate intranet or the help desk's main site.

o   Be sure to speak with HR about including this "help desk handbook" as part of new employee orientation.

5. **Maintain ongoing visibility of the help desk.** Once the bridge has been established between you and the end

users, it will need constant care to avoid falling into disrepair again. Stay in users' faces! For example, considering launching a weekly help desk update in the form of a newsletter or article. Include information like:

o   Changes in help desk procedures, technologies, or services.
o   Tips and tricks for end users.
o   Metrics and statistics of help desk performance.
o   Security alerts, bugs, and other problems, as well as workarounds and patches.

In Summary

Your help desk is too important a service (and too large an investment) to sit on the sidelines. Embark on a help desk marketing campaign to reinvigorate end-user enthusiasm.

How to Calculate Intangible Assets

As paradoxical as it sounds, sometimes proving the value of IT means looking at what's missing from the balance sheet rather than what's on it. Learn how to calculate "intangible" IT assets and gain a valuable tool for proving IT's worth to the company.

What Are Intangible Assets?

Intangible assets are non-physical, non-financial company resources or intellectual property that add to the organization's value and bottom line. From a broader business perspective, intangible assets include, but are not limited to: research and development, customer information and contacts, brand equity, goodwill, and so on.

In the case of IT proper, intangibles tend to focus on the strategic "fit" of IT investments, the return on those IT investments, opportunity costs, innovation, and the value derived from IT better serving its customers. More specifically, IT intangibles can be:

- Direct competitive advantage created through the innovative application of IT.
- Proprietary aspects of IT/business applications.
- Patent and copyright protection of proprietary applications.

How Big Is the Problem?

In IT and business alike, there have always been reluctance and aversion to placing quantitative numbers on qualitative things. According to a survey conducted by Accenture:

- 50 percent of respondents asserted that intangibles are "the primary source of long-term shareholder wealth creation" for their companies.

- 95 percent of respondents cited having a poor system for measuring the performance of intangible assets.
- 33 percent said they had no system at all for measuring the performance of intangible assets.

If intangible assets are so important, then why are they so hard to measure? Business Finance Magazine offers two possible reasons. One states that intangible assets are so numerous and vague that executives end up using guesswork to select those non-financial items that they *think* drive value. The second reason is that there are no widely accepted standards for estimating intangibles, and companies therefore have little or no guidance in this area.

What's at Stake?
Some will argue that intangible assets are just as important as tangible assets when it comes to creating shareholder value. Others insist that intangibles have no place on the balance sheet, which is the first document that potential investors look for. What side of this fence does your CEO sit on? How about the Board? Find out the views held by these two very important corporate entities, as this will put you in a better position to shape your findings accordingly.

Action Plan
If you've been tasked to demonstrate and/or valuate IT intangibles, read the following points to develop a better understanding of such a process.

1. **Use the calculated intangible value (CIV) method.** Investopedia.com advocates the CIV formula for identifying intangible assets that produce earnings. Start by finding out your company's average pre-tax net income for the last three years. Let's use $50 million as an example.
2. **Dig up some balance sheets** for those same three years, and obtain from them your company's average year-end tangible assets. Let's assume this figure is

$250 million. To calculate return on assets (ROA), divide the net income figure by the tangible assets figure: $50 million ÷ $250 million = 20 percent.

3. **Now find out the average ROA for your industry.** Continuing with our example, let's say the average ROA for the widget manufacturing industry is 12 percent. You have to multiply the industry ROA by your company's tangible assets, and subtract from that total the company's pre-tax net income. In this case: 12 percent x $250 million - $50 million = $20 million excess ROA.

4. **Subtract taxes.** Find out what the average income tax rate was for the three years under review. Using an example tax rate of 33 percent, multiply it by the excess ROA number and subtract the result from the original excess ROA number to come up with an after-tax figure: 33 percent x $20 million - $20 million = $13.4 million in after-tax excess ROA. This final number is known as the "premium."

5. **Calculate the net present value (NPV) of the premium.** Divide the discount rate for the company's cost of capital by the premium. Let's use an arbitrary number for the discount rate, at 15 percent (be sure to ask your Finance department about this to get a firm number). The total value of the company's intangible assets is therefore almost *$90 million* ($13.4 million ÷ 15 percent = $89.3 million). This is the number that should go on the balance sheet under Intangible Assets; in other words, a properly-calculated, hard number that accurately depicts assets' value.

6. **Calculate how IT contributes to the total value of intangible assets.** Quality of service, convenience of new processes, timeliness, and increased productivity: all of these are IT-specific intangibles. Solicit feedback from users to find out where your strengths lie. There is no hard-and-fast formula to calculate the value of IT intangibles, as they differ from company to company.

In Summary

Intangible assets can make or break your company, so don't fall victim to omitting them during your IT valuation efforts.

How to Develop an IT Operations Plan

Every couple of years, most IT managers or CIOs have to face the burdensome task of conducting IT operations planning for their respective organizations. This is a really big deal, so make sure you understand everything that must go into an IT operations plan.

What Is an IT Operations Plan?

An IT operations plan is a one-year, highly-detailed tactical plan for implementing the objectives of a higher-level strategic IT plan. The operations plan uses a technical architecture as a guide for development and integration of these objectives and the systems they affect.

The IT operations plan should also include a two to five year plan for evaluating the success and value of the one-year tactical objectives in order to ascertain how they may be implemented elsewhere in the organization. Additionally, the plan must:

- Annually be updated and submitted to senior management.
- Include a detailed description of the organization's requirements and budgets, as well as plans for information systems for each organizational element.
- Contain information system requirements and accompanying budget initiatives as they relate to the organization's mission statement.
- Have user requirements translated into realistic, cost-effective, and well-coordinated plans that tie together common requirements into a cohesive, organization-wide plan.
- Ensure that acquisitions of information systems are in accordance with the updated IT operations plan.

Action Plan

If you haven't been mandated to produce an IT operations plan, you may want to start on one anyway. Be sure to take these steps and include the following information when creating your own IT operations plan.

1. **Executive summary.** The executive summary is a top-level introduction to your plan. In it, you may wish to include broad details, such as the timeframe covered by the plan (e.g. 2008 to 2009), a brief listing of the contents of the document, or a flowchart that graphically depicts how your tactical plan works.
2. **Overview of your existing infrastructure.** Provide an outline detailing the general state of the organization's technology infrastructure. Where applicable, describe any recent wins or successful initiatives from the IT department that have contributed value to the company (e.g. deployment of collaboration servers, data warehouse, etc.).
3. **Tactical objectives.** This is arguably the most difficult part of writing the plan, but definitely the most important. List the main points and make absolutely certain that tactical objectives map directly to strategic goals. For example, if a strategic goal for the 2008 to 2009 timeframe is to provide e-learning support for employees, then you must demonstrate how IT is going to tactically make that possible. Moving ahead with the e-learning example, a sample tactical objective could read like the following statement:
   - First-Year Tactic: "The IT department will plan a rollout of e-learning deployments by installing a digital white board in two of our five satellite offices, along with three PC-based teaching stations. Informational materials will be accessible from the main FTP server via a high-speed WAN link."
   - Second-Year Update: "The IT department will assess and evaluate the success of this initiative. Based on our findings and the continued feasibility of the plan, we will begin a staged rollout of e-learning initiatives to the remaining three offices."

4. **Capital costs and other numbers.** It's always a good idea to show the dollar value of existing IT capital. If, for example, your IT operations plan includes a section on, say, asset management, create a table that lists the replacement cost, net value, and depreciation amounts for all IT asset types.
5. **Budgets, funding, and forecasts.** Financial figures are also very important to include in your report. Provide detailed information on the following areas:
   o **Budgets** - Include all expenses for the years encapsulated by the plan, especially salaries, hardware, software, supplies, infrastructure, staff development, and so on. Be sure to give your best estimates for the three- or five-year projection.
   o **Funding** - Summarize any pre-allocated, ongoing, and one-time funding for current IT projects, as well as proposed projects. Include a short, two-sentence paragraph for each project that falls under one of these three headings.
   o **Forecasts** - Outline your proposed financial forecasts for the time period covered by the plan. Summarize average annual spending expected for operations, maintenance, depreciation, capital works, and so on.
6. **Keep the plan current.** Revisit your plan at least once per quarter and measure your accomplishments against it, but only update it once per year - constantly modifying the plan is counterproductive to the plan itself.

In Summary

An IT operations plan is an excellent way to provide your department with a practical, tactical series of steps and guidelines for the next few years. Take the time to do it right.

How to Monitor Cash Flow

Cash is the lifeblood of any company. In order to assess your company's financial position, as well as the viability of potential vendors and business partners, it is essential to analyze how cash flows in and out of the business. Learn to read a statement of cash flow to improve IT decision making.

Documenting the Sources and Uses of Cash

The cash flow statement reports a company's sources and uses of cash, as well as the beginning and ending cash values during a specified period. It also includes the combined total change in cash from all sources and uses of cash.

Cash includes currency, checks on hand, and bank deposits. Cash equivalents are highly liquid short-term investments, including treasury bills, or certificates of deposit. There are three key numbers in the cash flow statement that illustrate the results of cash transactions, in three categories:

1. **Net cash provided (or used) by operating activities.** This number tells how much cash a company's operations generate or use. It includes important items from the following consolidated financial statements:
   - Income statement:
     - Net earnings (profit or loss).
     - Depreciation expense.
   - Balance sheet (impact on cash flow):
     - Inventory changes (increases = use of cash / decreases = source of cash).
     - Accounts receivable changes (increases = use of cash / decreases = source of cash).
     - Accounts payable changes (increases = source of cash / decreases = use of cash).
2. **Net cash provided (or used) by investing activities.** This number tells how much cash the company has used to buy (or has received) from sales of stock, assets, and businesses. An example of an investing activity is renovating an office.

3. **Net cash provided (or used) by financing activities.** This number tells how much cash the company received from or paid to creditors or stockholders. Examples of financing activities are: paying dividends to share profits with stockholders; buying back stock from stockholders; and repaying creditors.

Action Plan

Use the following steps to help you analyze a cash flow statement.

1. **Study a cash flow statement.** Ask the finance department for a copy of your cash flow statement (if possible). As an alternative, or for additional practice, choose three or four public companies that are of interest to you. Go to the investments area on their Web sites. The cash flow statement is located in the annual report with the other consolidated financial statements.
2. **Determine if operating activities are generating cash.** Begin your investigation of the cash flow statement by looking at the company's operating activities. Keep the following tips in mind during your investigation:
    o   It is a positive sign if the company has generated cash from their operations. Operating cash flow can only be sustained for limited time periods. It is not automatically a bad sign if they have not. If cash is not being generated from operating activities, investigate which working capital components are using large sums of cash and think about what the company might be doing.
    o   For example, if a company has purchased another company during the statement period, you will likely see a large use of cash. Provided the acquired inventory can increase future cash flows, this is a good sign, even though the company's operating activities did not generate positive cash flow.
3. **Examine the cash provided for or used in investing activities.** Compare the current year's capital expenditures to the previous year's capital expenditures. Note any significant increases or decreases. Does this shed any additional light on your initial ideas about the company's financial position? For example:

- A reduction in capital expenditures might indicate that the company has bank constraints or cash flow problems.
- An increase in capital expenditures could be a warning sign for future financial difficulties if they are stretching their creditors to fund recent acquisitions.
4. **Examine the cash provided by, or used in, financing activities.** This section tells you how much debt or equity the company has used or repaid.
- Did they use financing as a cash source or did they use cash to pay down their line of credit?
- Did they use any unusual financing activities not highlighted elsewhere in the analysis?
5. **Keep it simple.** The preceding steps can be summarized by asking the following questions when performing a cash flow analysis:
- How much cash was generated from operating activities?
- From cash generated, how much was invested?
- How much was used to pay down debt, or how did debt increase?
6. **Learn how to read other financial statements.** Analysts often use a cash flow statement in conjunction with a balance sheet and an income statement when performing financial analyses. These can come in handy when you are trying to understand the financial condition of prospective vendors or business partners.

In Summary

Cash flow analysis will help you determine how effectively a company generates and manages its cash. Be sure you can properly analyze cash flow statements.

Information Lifecycle Management

Many enterprises are in the midst of consolidation projects that are resulting in significant data growth, as well as compliance initiatives that require the retention of more data for longer periods of time. Have a look at Information Lifecycle Management (ILM) as a way to help improve the efficiency with which data is used. Even if you're not currently ready to deploy ILM, educate yourself in the technologies and processes involved so you can capitalize on ILM in the future.

Fundamentals of ILM

ILM is a combination of technologies and processes that determines how data flows through an environment. With that in mind, here are some functions of ILM that add value:

- Reclaims space on storage resources like SANs, which are costly.
- Allows you to differentiate reference data from production data.
- Enables the study of data reuse and data retrieval patterns.
- Provides structured control over file deletion and retention decisions.
- Assists in maintaining compliance with mandated government regulations, and optimizes data protection and information availability.
- Maintains application transparency, as executives don't have time to concern themselves with data's whereabouts.

Storage Management Technologies

There are many possible storage management technologies that can play a role in ILM. Here are two:

- **SRM (Storage Resource Management)** technology helps the system administrator figure out what data resides on company storage assets by generating reports that outline data usage patterns.
- **ADM (Automated Data Migration)** technology is essentially a combination of intelligent SRM and HSM (Hierarchical Storage Management). HSM is access-driven, and was designed to automate data migration for archival purposes. ADM is different because it is data-value-driven and allows data migration across various storage resources, based on a combination of user identified criteria. Quality ADM tools assist IT in assigning value to the storage assets.

Action Plan

Data growth and manageability are major issues for larger enterprises, and likely these companies will be the first to adopt ILM. Small and medium-sized enterprises are expected to approach ILM in a piecemeal fashion. Familiarize yourself with the phases of ILM to enable complete implementation, or partial implementation endeavors.

1. **Assess the location of the data.** Use SRM (Storage Resource Management) technologies to enable your system administrator(s) to figure out what data resides on which storage assets.
2. **Socialize department heads.** Generate reports from the SRM tools to outline data usage patterns. Once your department has a better understanding

of what data it has and where it is located, this information should be shared with department heads by explaining the breakdown of storage asset utilization and related costs.

3. **Create a classification schema.** Continue to use SRM solutions to reveal duplicate or unnecessary files, excess capacity, or aged files. Prioritize the data based on business requirements from business units. This will help your department generate policies to migrate data to proper storage "classes" over time, and will illustrate where data should live throughout its lifecycle. You should classify your data in the following ways:
   o   Data organization.
   o   Data age.
   o   Data type.
   o   Data value.

4. **Automate migration of data.** Once a plan has been created for where data should live at every point in its lifecycle, and policies are established, investigate ADM (Automated Data Migration) tools. Use ADM tools to automate the migration of data from one class to another based on the policies generated. Assist system administrators with establishing criteria surrounding the data based on ownership, type, age, and when it was last accessed.

5. **Review the ILM process.** IT must continually review the usage patterns of its storage resources and ensure adherence to procedures and policies. By taking advantage of the SRM/ADM tools, monitoring the process becomes a lot easier.

In Summary

Evaluate your organizations storage needs. If your organization is not yet ready to implement ILM, at the very least stay on top of the technologies and get yourself in the mindset of the ILM principles. ILM will become increasingly important as your organization becomes more involved in disaster recovery, business continuity planning, and compliance with regulatory guidelines for storage.

IT Benchmarking

Industry benchmarks provide valuable reference points for IT decision makers trying to gauge their department's performance. Use these powerful tools to rally required resources, quantify the value of your department, and improve performance.

What Is Benchmarking?

The word "benchmark" means "to take a measurement against a reference point." From an IT perspective, it is a process of industrial research that enables the IT decision maker to compare key metrics of his/her organization to industry norms. This process of comparison helps IT decision makers identify processes and practices that can contribute to optimal service levels, and make IT a strategic enabler for the business.

The Benefits of Benchmarking

Industry benchmarking can provide IT managers with answers to the following key questions:

- What is your revenue/IT budget ratio with respect to other industry peers?
- How are industry peers staffing their departments?
- What are the top spending priorities?
- What is the outlook for IT spending in your industry: flat, increasing, or decreasing?
- How does your IT staff turnover rate compare to the industry average?
- What is an appropriate IT staff/employee ratio for your industry and company size?

Finding the answers to these questions goes a long way towards helping IT decision makers assess their internal operations and the overall health of the organization. This is critical information when business leaders ask about IT spending levels and how the department can add more value to the business.

Budgeting and staffing benchmarks can help IT create a noticeable impact on a variety of organizational activities, including:

- Justifying expenditures.
- Meeting user requirements.
- Setting relevant, achievable goals.
- Developing measures of productivity.
- Becoming competitive.
- Adopting industry best practices.

The Benchmarking Process

The best benchmarking processes are customized to suit the needs of individual organizations. Failure to take this into consideration often results in failure. A successful benchmarking process is typically based on the following six steps:

1. **Gather internal and external quantitative data.** Select the measurements to be benchmarked and prepare easily-understood comparison charts. The data itself, plus charts, graphs, and comments, can be used for this purpose. Document the relevance of each factor to the company and its operations.
2. **Determine current performance gaps.** Once all the data is in, compare against industry benchmarks. This will reveal any performance gaps between the department's operations and industry norms. Review comments to identify any contextual information that helps qualify discrepancies between internal results and industry benchmarks. This will include innovative practices and unique approaches.
3. **Communicate benchmark findings.** Present and promote the benchmarking results in order to win support for change.

4. **Establish functional goals.** Based on your findings, make recommendations for change to senior management.
5. **Develop action plans.** With benchmarks, objectives, and action plans in place, the transformation can begin. Monitor progress and report rising performance levels to all affected.
6. **Recalibrate benchmarks.** Because market forces and business practices constantly change, plan to re-evaluate and recalibrate your benchmarks at set intervals.

In Summary

Industry benchmarks are invaluable tools for helping an IT department locate strengths and weaknesses, and identify corrective actions. Add benchmarking to your management toolkit and improve your management profile.

IT Change Management the Negatives

Effective IT change management plays an important role in protecting the business operation. IT managers who are establishing a formal IT change management process in their enterprise must be prepared for the costs and pitfalls described in this research note.

IT Change Management Defined

IT change management is the process of controlling the creation and introduction of changes into the IT environment to minimize service disruptions. According to the IT Infrastructure Library (ITIL), "the goal of the change management process is to ensure that standardized methods and procedures are used for efficient and prompt handling of all changes, in order to minimize the impact of change-related incidents upon service quality, and consequently improve the day-to-day operations of the organization."

In terms of the process itself, change management is responsible for:

- Logging changes.
- Assessing the impact, cost, benefit, and risk of requested changes.
- Providing approval or rejection.
- Overseeing the change implementation.
- Monitoring and reporting the status of change.
- Closing change requests and conducting post-implementation reviews.

The Costs of a Formal Change Management Process

There are two main costs associated with establishing a formal change management process:

Staff costs. The organization of a formal change management process requires the creation of a new

67

role: the change manager. This person will be responsible for facilitating the adoption of the new process across the enterprise and for managing the process once it is in place. The company's size and volume of change dictate whether this new function requires full or part-time dedication. Small and mid-size companies don't need a full-time person dedicated to this role. They can assign this part-time function to an existing business systems analyst, to the help desk leader, or to another key support person in the team. Large companies need a full-time person dedicated to this role.

Automated tools. Companies that implement a formal change management process often need to buy or build tools to automate and support the process. The type of tool depends on the size of the organization and the volume and type of changes that need to be made. There are three approaches that companies can use to get automated tools:

- **Buy an IT Service Management suite.** These tools integrate support for Change Management, Configuration Management, Problem Management, and Service Desk processes of the ITIL Service Management framework. These tools are more expensive but the additional cost is justifiable for large enterprises or for *mid-sized companies with a high volume of changes to manage.*
- **Buy a change management solution.** These tools are usually one module of an entire IT Service Management suite and address only the specific requirements of the change management process. Investing in this tool is less expensive but it only addresses the change management needs. This option is recommended for *Small or Midsized Enterprises (SMEs) with high volume of changes to manage* (i.e. more than 100 change requests per month).
- **Build a solution.** Companies that can't afford a commercial change management solution can automate their process using existing tools. This

automation doesn't require a large development effort and it will greatly improve the efficiency of the change management process. Examples of internal tools to use for the automation include e-mail software (e.g. MS Exchange, Lotus Notes), development/database tools (e.g. Visual Basic, MS Access), and collaboration tools (e.g. SharePoint has templates for change management). This option is recommendable for SMEs with low or medium volume of changes to manage (i.e. fewer than 100 change requests per month).

Pitfalls to Watch

Enterprises that implement a formal change management process must be aware of the following pitfalls and respond appropriately:

Pitfall	Mitigation Strategy
Senior management doesn't support the change management process. As a result, users resist using the process.	The head of the IT department must meet with the heads of the business units to get their buy-in. The way to get this buy-in is to explain the need for a process by using examples of actual issues that have created business disruptions. Another powerful reason to get senior management buy-in is compliance. Regulatory requirements such as Sarbanes-Oxley or HIPAA require a formal change management process that protects critical IT applications and infrastructure.
There is no clear business or IT ownership of the systems impacted by the change. This often results in delays and incomplete assessments of the	Spend sufficient time upfront getting senior management buy-in and developing a solid change management policy that clearly identifies roles and responsibilities for each application and infrastructure component.

change.

The change management process is too bureaucratic and slow. As a result, the business won't follow it.	The process must maintain a balance between formality and practicality. Remember that the ultimate purpose of the process is to improve the quality of the IT services. Address this issue in two ways: 1. **Fix the process.** Meet with key business users and identify bottlenecks and unnecessary steps. Tune up the process as required and get business signoff before re-deploying it. Communicate to the organization accordingly and provide training in the new process. 2. **Automate.** Buy or build tools to automate and speed up the process. This will make life easier for both the user community and the IT department.
The authorization of minor changes takes more time than the implementation itself.	Provide the change manager with the authority to directly approve and prioritize minor changes.
The process fails when emergency changes are requested.	This happens because most of the typical members of the Change Advisory Board (CAB) (i.e. decision makers) are unavailable to meet immediately in response to an urgent request. Create a smaller team (usually called CAB/Emergency Committee) to handle emergency requests. Work with the business to identify one individual for each application who is empowered with the authority to make quick decisions.

	These individuals plus the change manager will be the members of the CAB/EC.
The change management process is not integrated with other processes. For example, the impact of changes on documentation and training is often overlooked.	In the request for change (RFC) form, specifically include fields that clearly identify the impact of the change on existing applications, infrastructure, business continuity, and contingency plans. Follow ITIL best practices to integrate IT change management with other IT processes including configuration management and release management.

Recommendations

1. **Don't rush to get a tool, establish the process first.** Using automated tools to support change management is important but getting senior management support and establishing a solid change management process must precede the consideration of tools.
2. **Make it practical.** The purpose of creating a formal change management process is to deliver IT services in a faster, less risky, and more effective way. Be formal and organized but avoid creating bureaucratic steps that may slow down the process and frustrate the business.

In Summary

IT managers must not rush to get a tool to automate IT change management. Instead, they must make sure they have strong senior management support and a solid and practical process.

IT Governance the Basics

For standardizing IT processes, simplifying operations, aligning IT with business, and cutting costs, nothing works quite as well as IT governance. Start improving these and other areas by changing your current IT structures within the crucible of a governance model.

What Is IT Governance?

At the macro level, successful IT governance is accomplished by basing IT practices on high-quality, well-defined, repeatable processes. At the micro level, IT governance focuses on developing precise policies, clearly defined procedures, and scrupulously detailed documentation. In addition to zeroing in on these areas, IT governance also constitutes a forward-looking plan for continual improvement.

Types of Governance Models

There are two main public models for IT governance. The **IT Infrastructure Library (ITIL)** is a widely accepted approach. Specifically developed for IT service management and operations, ITIL is a framework of best practices that are documented in an abstract fashion to be applicable to any IT organization. ITIL's main focus is to provide service objectives, key activities, and key performance indicators for applications management, IT service delivery and support, infrastructure management, and business perspectives. This method is divided into 48 modules/processes.

Elsewhere, the **Control Objectives for Information and related Technology (COBIT)** is used as a control framework for corporate IT processes. Organizations use COBIT to manage accountability of IT resources, focus resources on business goals, and to build a framework for risk assessment. It divides information technology into 34 modules/processes that are further organized into four domains: planning, acquiring and implementing, delivery and support, and monitoring.

Action Plan

1. **Get executives on board.** IT governance is a control management system that enables you to translate a strategic vision into practical and measurable actions. If the top executives don't understand and support a strategic framework for IT governance, then the outcome won't have value. Also, governance is embedded in organizational culture and politics, not just processes. Backing from the C-level team is therefore critical.

2. **Know what you're working towards.** Reviews of successful IT governance models have revealed that there are characteristics common to all models. Derived from industry standards, the following outcomes are indicative, but not exhaustive, of well-executed governance deployments:

   o Complete, flexible IT structure geared toward the delivery of business applications.

   o Centrally managed IT infrastructure, as well as centralized IT staff.

   o Estimated project costs based on a five-year lifecycle cost.

   o Project portfolio management in place.

   o Clearly defined reporting relationships and strict adherence to standards.

3. **Use modules from the standards bodies.** An IT shop in a mid-sized company won't be able to implement ITIL or COBIT in whole - they are simply too big and all-encompassing. You can, however, use parts of them that speak directly to your particular needs. For example, if the help desk is your worry, then use the help desk module from ITIL like the government of Ontario did. When using this module-by-module approach, keep the following tips in mind:

   o Be sure to first benchmark the trouble area before moving ahead with the module. This way, you will be able to better measure performance over time.

   o Continue to stay focused on this one area of change, as training, implementation, and change management will pose major ongoing challenges.

- Use such projects as a learning experience. Document everything and use this information when moving on to the next area that could use governance.
4. **Tie in governance with compensation.** Management must lead the charge when implementing IT governance. Bonus programs for employees will have to change to reflect a focus on positive metrics and key performance indicator improvements.

In Summary

IT governance plays an important role in making companies more successful via streamlined and standardized processes. Get started now to realize long-term benefits.

IT Value Defined

The task of communicating IT value is critical for CIOs looking to justify expenditures, raise the profile of IT in the organization, and ensure that resources are being allocated appropriately. However, before you can communicate the importance of IT to the rest of the organization, you must first define what "IT value" really means and determine if the approach you are taking to calculate it is the correct one.

Value Methodologies Exposed

The notion of IT value has changed dramatically. In part because of the "irrational exuberance" of the dot-com years and the more recent embarrassment of corporate scandals, IT value has come under increased scrutiny. Where it was once sufficient to demonstrate ROI or measure TCO, numerous value methodologies have since emerged that look beyond one dimensional financial measures.

Despite the differences among the various methods, a common belief does exist that cost reduction, system upgrades, implementations, and data creation, do not in and of themselves create value.

We also know that as IT functions are consolidated and centralized, IT value becomes increasingly difficult to quantify because it becomes less clear which resources are being used to enable which business functions. Additionally, we know that in order to accurately identify value drivers, complete transparency of business and IT operations is needed.

Consider the following commonly used ways to identify IT value:

- ***Traditional, financial measures:*** These include measures such as Return on Investment (ROI), Net Present Value (NPV), Internal Rate of Return (IRR), and payback period. While valuable, these measures tend to be one dimensional and do not properly communicate long term benefits or strategic value. They also do not show an awareness of business objectives, fail to incorporate the business risk associated with new investments (i.e. they usually portray a best case scenario), and tend to foster less collaboration among business units. In most cases, the key driver in these types of models is maximizing bottom line profitability.

- *Multidimensional measures:* The Balanced Scorecard and Earned Value Analysis (EVA) are good measures in that they take a more holistic approach to measure the impact of IT on the business; however, these complex performance models are often cumbersome and difficult to implement, maintain, and re-evaluate on an ongoing basis.

- *Classification measures:* These can be good ways of categorizing value drivers, but must be looked at through the lens of business objectives. As an example, value could be broken down into automational, informational, or transformational drivers.

  o Automation drivers reduce labor costs and error rates, and can improve productivity.

  o Informational drivers capture, interpret, and disseminate information, leading to better decision-making, analysis of performance metrics, and efficiency.

  o Transformational drivers that change a business model through technology alone are rare, but are possible to achieve, as in the case of e-commerce applications that lead to large changes in market share.

Value vs. Benefits vs. Features

Often, managers confuse IT value with creating new features, or identifying the benefits of a new initiative. It is important to understand the difference.

- *Feature:* This is simply a capability of a product or service.
- *Benefit:* A feature that solves a problem or helps improve usability, productivity, or profitability is a benefit.

While we can say that things are "better," this is still not a quantifiable measure of value.

- *Value:* Value is created when a significant benefit is measurable and actionable, can be expressed in monetary terms, leads to competitive advantage, is traceable over time, and fulfills a particular business need. Another way of looking at it is the ability to positively affect key performance indicators (i.e. measurable indicators that will be used to report progress towards the key success factors of the company).

Action Plan

IT value is elusive and often confused with features or benefits. Use the following tips to help get to the heart of the matter and define the IT value drivers in your organization.

1. **Consider what your CEO means by "creating value."** Value creation aims at maximizing the following:
   o Doing the right work, based on aligning IT investments with business strategy.
   o Doing the right work faster by improving productivity, standardizing workflows, and automating business processes.
   o Using the right resources and properly managing people, capital, business partners, and IT assets.
   o Doing the work correctly, through knowledge sharing, proper information management, and shared processes and templates.
   o Improving organizational transparency and control measures to identify and solve problems early.
2. **Don't build functionality without understanding the underlying need.** Generating new functionality or implementing a new system does not create value unless that function or capability fulfills a specific business need or creates some sort of lasting competitive advantage. Also, don't be fooled by vendors claiming that their products make it easier to achieve value. These claims are likely marketing hype, especially

since the companies selling you their products don't know what your business goals are.

3. **Link IT value to business objectives.**

o   Start by prioritizing your company's business objectives to identify areas where IT can make the biggest improvements. Is the company's focus on customer service, new product development, sales growth, order processing, or knowledge management?

o   Next, identify the key success factors that enable this business objective and the key performance indicators that are used to measure these success factors. Key success factors are the most important factors affecting the realization of strategic objectives and the success of the business.

o   Ask yourself how technology can be implemented to help improve these indicators. For instance, if the business objective is low cost development, then IT value needs to be defined in terms of cost control, productivity, and efficiency. In contrast, if the objective is greater market share through innovation and product differentiation, then IT value needs to be defined in terms of new customer acquisition or sales per customer.

4. **Track your performance.** A big part of creating value is being able to track your accomplishments over time. Look at historical performance and track your progress towards the ultimate goal.

In Summary

Value is not simply a list of benefits. Determine what needs to be done to properly identify the value created by your IT shop.

Leader or Manager

Managing a team or department requires a combination of skills working in concert - leadership is one of these skills. However, not all managers are leaders and not all leaders are managers. Learn to distinguish between the two: it will make the difference between success and failure.

Leaders vs. Managers

People often make the erroneous assumption that all managers by default have leadership abilities. The truth is that leadership skills and managerial skills don't describe two different people, but rather represent opposite ends of the "boss" spectrum. To showcase this spectrum refer to the table of attributes listed below:

Leader	Manager
Innovator	Administrator
-Develops and creates	-Maintains
-Questions reality	-Accepts reality
-Focuses on people	-Focuses on systems and structures
-Sees the long-term	-Sees the short-term
-Asks what and why	-Asks how and when
-Always has one eye on the horizon	-Always has one eye on the bottom line
-Challenges the status quo	-Accepts the status quo
Is his or her own person	Is the classic "good soldier"

Action Plan

1. **Consult the attributes table.** You must, in all honesty to yourself, conclude whether you're a manager or a leader. A person who exhibits all the traits in the right-hand manager column and none from the left is very rigid and unlikely to change. If you're looking to build your leadership skills, then the column on the left is

where you want to be. Just remember that managing is what you do with tasks, while leading is what you do with people. Proficiency with the former will help you excel at the latter.

2. **Be comfortable with what you are.** If you're a manager and not a leader, simply realizing that about yourself is an excellent first step. This does not mean you're a failure - it just means that a particular skill set isn't as honed as it could be. Chances are that one of your subordinates is the unofficial leader of your team or department - enlist this person's help to assist you in leading the group.

3. **It's all about the employees.** As mentioned earlier, leading is what you do with people. The actual work notwithstanding, being a leader means stepping up to the plate for your workers in all situations. This results in a huge morale boost for your employees, as they know that no matter what happens, you, their leader, will always be in their corner. Where the work itself is concerned, be an equal contributor to the effort at hand: equally responsible and actively involved in your team's success.

4. **Don't go overboard.** Developing leadership skills is obviously desirable for anyone in a managerial position, but this should never be done at the expense of your effective manager skills (which are critical for getting things done). Both skill sets are important to organizations. If you can't be 100 percent at both roles, settle for a happy medium, or risk creating a potential skills gap.

5. **Use additional resources.** There are literally thousands upon thousands of self-help Web sites, consulting groups, courses, and workshops you can look at for learning leadership abilities.

In Summary

Being a great manager goes a long way toward laying the foundation of a good leader. Just remember not to sacrifice the one to make room for the other in your skill set.

Lease vs. Buy Determined Using TVM

IT decision makers are required to make expensive multiyear purchases. Calculate the present value of future payment options to inform your purchase decision and earn C level credibility.

Time Value of Money: The Basic Idea

Given the option of receiving $10,000 today or $10,000 three years from now, most people would choose option A. Why would you wait if you could have the same amount now? Instinctively this makes sense, but understanding the financial math behind the time value of money (TVM) can help us solve more complicated decisions. The underlying premise behind time value is that the value of money changes over time. Over the course of three years, the future value (FV) of the first option will be $10,000 plus any interest acquired over the three years.

In the real world, the more likely application of the TVM is minimizing cash outflows over a multi-year period. We face these decisions every day. Whether it's deciding to buy or lease a car, putting a 10% or 20% down payment on a house, or choosing a fixed or variable mortgage rate, we often look for the least expensive option.

Calculating Present Value

Unlike the first example where we looked at the impact of compounding interest on future values, comparing payment options requires calculating the present value (PV) of future cash outflows. To find PV, or the amount that we would have to invest today, you must subtract the accumulated interest from the FV. To achieve this, we can discount the future payment amount by the interest rate for the period. In the previous example, finding the PV of option B requires discounting $10,000 by the interest compounded over a three year period.

Consider the following example: An enterprise with a PC refresh rate of four years has 15 computers at the end of their lifecycle. Assuming a discount rate of 5%, which of the following two payment options should the IT decision maker take?

- **Option A.** Make an $8,000 payment at the beginning of year 1 and an $8,000 payment at the beginning of year 3.
- **Option B.** Make four annual payments of $4,000 starting at the beginning of year 1.

Option B with a PV of $14,892.99 costs less than option A with a PV of $14,910.70. If the decision was based solely on the PV of a four-year purchase plan, option B is a better choice. However, purchasing decisions are rarely this simple. The impact of cash flow on the IT budget is of equal, if not more, importance. For example, after a three-year period, in option A there is a cash outflow of $8,000, compared to $12,000 in option B.

Recommendations

1. **Use a calculator.** Use a present value calculator to evaluate the impact of any future payment option on current cash flow.
2. **Find the corporate discount rate.** The most difficult part of a PV calculation is finding the appropriate discount rate. The premise behind the discount rate is calculating the opportunity cost of an IT investment compared to a capital market investment in such as stock, treasury bills, and bonds. Talk to the finance department to find out what rate you should use.
3. **Know the limitations of a PV calculation.** When PV is properly used, it is a powerful tool that allows the IT decision maker to assess a project based on the a TVM. It is also important to recognize its shortcomings:
   - It does not measure profitability.

- o For projects without a concrete start and end date (like a lease), it requires an arbitrary cutoff point and ignores cash flows beyond the cutoff date.
- o Requires companies to determine an optimal discount rate.

Finding the Discount

PV is calculated using the formula PV = FV / (1 + i)n - 1, where:
o FV = future value.
o i = discount rate.
o n = time period.

The discount rate used in a PV calculation is the rate of return that your company could generate if it was not invested in the selected project.

Most finance departments have a designated discount rate for calculating the TVM over multi-year payment plans.

It is also referred to as a hurdle rate or the cost of capital.

In Summary

Go beyond technical justification when making purchase decisions. Use present value calculations to be more credible and professional with executives.

Mergers & Acquisitions

If you walk into your office tomorrow morning to news that your company has purchased or merged with another company, or has itself been bought out, would you know where to begin your post-merger tasks? If an unexpected merger or acquisition happens to you, start building a checklist now to ensure you make it through the critical first few days without undue stress.

IT's Integration Destiny

Companies are bought and sold all the time. No matter which side you're on, the impact of a merger or acquisition on IT can be huge. Beyond the need to integrate existing systems and plan for a combined future IT strategy, managers need to bring two sets of IT staff together. That's not always easy when most employees might fear for their jobs. Worse, IT managers can often be the last to know about an impending consolidation, which leaves them scrambling for answers when the news finally breaks.

Action Plan

Make sure your checklist contains the following key elements to help you survive your first post-merger day.

1. **Know where you stand.** Your role within the merger will vary significantly depending on how the deal played out. Confirm which side of the fence you currently occupy; if you are on the receiving end, your role may be diminished compared to managers on the dominant side. There are three typical merger/acquisition scenarios, each with their own unique impacts on your job:
   o Your company did the buying - this puts you in a stronger position.
   o Both companies merged equally - this puts you in a competitive situation.
   o Your company was bought - this puts you in a weaker position.

2. **Identify and prioritize the expected benefits of the merger or acquisition as they apply to IT.** Most mergers are driven by the potential to save money, much of which will be realized by IT. IT is on the hook to deliver these savings, and you will be measured on how you achieve them. Lay out a definitive roadmap now to maximize your potential for success. Some potential saving strategies include:
o   Staff reduction.
o   Facility and technology consolidation.
o   Reduction in software inventory through selection of dominant or best-of-breed applications.
3. **Pull all relevant documentation.** Know who's who, what's what, and how to quickly look up all information that will be critical to the integration. Identify source locations and key personnel responsible for the following:
o   Organizational charts.
o   Hardware/software inventories.
o   Project inventory.
o   Skills inventories and staffing assignments.
4. **Confirm your message.** Get your facts straight before you speak to anyone. Challenge your own leaders to outline everything they know, and what can and cannot be divulged at this time. But do it quickly before the rumor mill takes over and adds to your Day One headaches.
5. **Find your shadow.** Successful integration depends on key staff members from each company reaching out to each other to form working partnerships. Identify your other-company counterpart and call on him or her to get the relationship started immediately.
6. **Schedule and hold meetings with your leadership group.** To maximize visibility to all employees, meetings should happen within the physical IT area, not offsite. Use a waterfall-type communication plan to ensure your messages are precisely delivered in a minimum amount of time. Once you've met with your leadership group, have each leader meet with his or her respective team.
7. **Visibly log questions.** This is a period of high uncertainty. Do everything you can to cut through the fog. Actively capture any questions that are posed during

meetings. Distribute an e-mail to all staff outlining how questions about the consolidation's impact are to be submitted, and what will happen to them afterward.

8. **Document your communication plan.** Decide what you will say, how often you will say it, at what level of detail, and in which medium. Share this with the rest of the department. Publish it on the corporate intranet and assign someone to maintain it in an evergreen state.

9. **Don't lose day-to-day control.** The pressures of integration make it easy to forget about IT's usual priorities of building, operating, and maintaining technology infrastructure, and of supporting bottom-line business requirements. Keep your pre-existing operational plans highly visible on this first day, and reinforce the importance of your staff maintaining a strong focus on business-as-usual support.

10. **Be a mentor.** Schedule some face-time toward the end of the day to assess the mood of your staff. They will let you know whether or not your initial post-merger activities are on the mark. They will also point you toward priorities for Day Two and beyond.

In Summary

For most people, it's only a matter of time before they're caught up in a corporate merger or acquisition. Like a good disaster recovery plan, get your plans in place now so you won't be swallowed up if and when a corporate coupling occurs.

Making Sure to Arm the IT Gladiator

When the gladiator goes into the arena to do battle, it's a good idea for them to bring along a sword and a shield. So, too, the IT gladiator needs a sword and shield. The shield is infrastructure and operations best practices. The sword is focused strategy.

The shield is the heavier and more unwieldy item. As an offensive weapon, it has little value. The sword is lighter and more nimble. But going into battle with just a sword leaves one dangerously exposed. Operations and infrastructure are time consuming and require heavy lifting. However, they ultimately play only a defensive role. You can't win the victory with just a shield. Poor practices, or no practices, will almost certainly guarantee defeat.

Network Security

For an example, take network security. Security management is a top priority for all IT shops. Huge amounts of time and money are expended on patch management, antivirus efforts, and access management. Yet for all that effort, security only "matters" when it fails. With security, the best news is no news. It is like that for nearly every area of operations and infrastructure. Do it well. Hit your targets. Nobody notices. Few care. But if there is a failure, everybody knows, and everybody cares.

There is another way in which operations and infrastructure management can lead to failure. Failure comes if these priorities require not just most, but all of the manager's time. I have seen IT gladiators who go into the arena with only a shield, blocking blow after blow until they collapse from exhaustion. These are the managers who spend all of their time keeping the wheels on the wagon and putting out the fires. They are unsung and unappreciated because success in operations and infrastructure is invisible.

The Importance of Good Practices

A survey of management and technology priorities of more than 1,400 IT decision makers in midsized enterprises found that a subgroup of the respondents were doing well on a number of key measures. Most had a productive relationship with the CEO and felt IT and business goals were well aligned. They were on top of their own schedule, and IT projects were consistently meeting expectations.

What are these high-achieving IT decision makers doing that underachievers are not? They are not necessarily getting or spending more money than other IT departments. So how are they different?

In 17 different areas of operations and infrastructure management, including security, disaster recovery planning, infrastructure planning, and staff training, the top performers scored much higher than underachievers in their attention to and execution of formal management systems.

What constitutes a formal system varies from area to area. It is generally a documented set of repeatable and measurable procedures or practices for executing on a specific management priority. The leading IT decision makers are executing well on management priorities across the board. This puts them in a good position to work with senior management on projects that will advance the business.

Think of the 80/20 rule, the axiom that at the end of the day 20% of the effort yields 80% of the benefit. The modern IT manager is besieged by competing priorities. Executing well across the board means that 80% of priorities are dealt with effectively and efficiently so that the IT manager can focus on the 20% that will make a difference.

First, No Harm

As a piece of IT management advice, "First, do everything well" sounds wishy washy and generally useless. It has a motherhood ring to it like "be polite." It comes off particularly lame when as the answer to a specific question, "What do I need to do well to excel as an IT manager?"

Everything? Thanks! That's so helpful. Note, however, that the advice is not just, "Do everything well." It is, "First, do everything well." This suggests that there is another proverbial piece of footwear to hit the floor. The other shoe goes thus: Second, focus on finding ways to use technology to grow the business - to help the enterprise get competitive advantage through forward-thinking IT investments. This is your sword.

You have probably heard this second piece of advice before. It relates to strategic goal setting and business alignment. Analysts, academics, and other assorted professional talkers have been telling IT managers for a quarter century that they need to focus on alignment.

In Summary

Most important is that the first piece of advice and the second piece of advice are mutually dependent. First, do everything well. Second, focus on alignment and business processes. They are like a one-two punch combination or a good shield and sword. Doing battle with one but not the other is like fighting with one hand tied behind your back.

Maximize Employee Performance with SL

Situational leadership is an effective model for managing and developing people. Improve the performance of your staff by learning to adapt your leadership style to different situations and different individuals.

Situational Leadership Defined

Ken Blanchard and Paul Hersey developed this theory at Ohio University in 1968. Essentially, situational leadership is a process for managers to maximize people's performance by adjusting their leadership style depending on the situation. The model is based upon a relationship between the subordinate's development level on a specific goal or task and the leadership style that the manager provides.

Why Use Situational Leadership?

Most managers have a predominant management style, which they use for every situation and with every employee. This approach is flawed and leads to ineffective management. The following table illustrates two examples of the negative consequences that result from not adapting the leadership style to the situation and to the individual.

Situation	Style Applied	Outcome/Consequences
A new project manager (PM) joins the company to lead an important initiative.	The manager's style is to always leave his employees alone and give them minimal support. In this case, he doesn't dedicate sufficient time to the new PM.	Although the new employee is very experienced in the PM discipline, he still doesn't understand the organization, its dynamics, and key players. Without his manager's support, the PM is not appropriately set up for success in leading such an important initiative. The result is an unsuccessful project and a frustrated employee who feels lost, helpless, and de-motivated.

		In the end, the PM ends up leaving the organization.
A senior consultant who has been with the company for a long time is assigned to work on a special project.	The project manager's style is to micromanage her people. In this case, she is constantly giving instructions and following up on the consultant's work.	The work gets done but not with the quality that the consultant usually delivers. The team environment is affected by internal conflicts that result from the consultant feeling that he is being treated as if he were incompetent.

IT managers who use situational leadership effectively can expect the following benefits:

- Better performance and faster career advancement for both their subordinates and themselves.
- Increases in job satisfaction and morale at all levels.
- Reductions in employee turnover and absenteeism.
- Overall organizational productivity improvements.

Profile the Development Cycle of Employees
According to the model, every individual is at one of four development levels as it relates to a specific task or assignment. Each development level is characterized by various combinations of competence and commitment. Figure 1 describes these levels.

The Four Development Levels of an Individual

LOW	MODERATE		HIGH
Low Competence High Commitment	Low to Some Competence Low Commitment	Moderate to High Competence Variable Commitment	High Competence High Commitment
D1 The Enthusiastic Beginner	D2 The Disillusioned Learner	D3 The Capable But Cautious Performer	D4 The Self-Reliant Achiever

Develop   _____ Develo
ing   ped

Individuals move sequentially forward through the above development cycle when matched with the appropriate situational leadership style.

Adopt a Leadership Style to Meet Development Levels

After a manager diagnoses the development level that the employee is at, he or she needs to determine what leadership style to apply for that level. The leadership styles are characterized by the amount of direction and support that the manager provides. When combining directive and supportive behavior, four leadership styles emerge, each one appropriate for one particular development level.

- **Style 1 – Directing.** The manager provides specific instructions about tasks and goals and closely supervises the employee's performance. This style is effective with an individual at D1 who needs strong direction and little support. In this style the manager makes most decisions.
- **Style 2 – Coaching.** The manager explains decisions, solicits suggestions from the employee, praises behaviors that are approximately right, and continues to direct task

accomplishment. This style is effective with an individual at D2 who needs direction to build competence and support to counter the drop in commitment. In this style, managers consider input from the individual but still make the final decisions.

- **Style 3 – Supporting.** The manager facilitates, listens, encourages ideas, and supports self-reliant decision making and problem solving. This style is effective with an individual at D3 who needs little direction but has motivational or confidence issues. In this style, the individual makes the final decisions but with input from the manager.
- **Style 4 – Delegating.** The manager empowers the employee to act independently and provides the appropriate resources to get the job done. This style is effective with an individual at D4 who needs low direction and low support. In this style, the individual makes most decisions.

The following are some examples of effective situational leadership as applied to some specific situations.

Situation	Development Level	Appropriate Leadership Style
New employee coming out from school with no professional experience.	D1 – Low competence and high Commitment.	S1 – Directing.
Experienced developer recently promoted to a management or project management position.	In relation to the management task, this person is in D1– Low competence and high commitment.	S1 – Directing.
Due to lack of technical resources, a development task is assigned to a business systems analyst.	D2 – Low to some competence and low commitment.	S2 – Coaching.
Java programmer who has been developing and supporting the same system for a long time.	D3 – High competence and low to mid commitment.	S3 – Supporting.
Certified Oracle DBA who is responsible for administering all of the company's Oracle Databases.	D4 – High competence and high commitment.	S4 – Delegating.
A highly experienced employee whose performance is being affected by a family crisis.	Normally it would be D4 but under these current circumstances it is D3 - High competence and low to mid commitment.	Manager must shift style from S4 – Delegating to S3 – Supporting.

Action Plan

1. **Take training.** Becoming a situational leader requires training and practice. Find out if the HR department has a training program about situational leadership. If they don't have anything, ask them to organize a session for the IT management team at least.
2. **Evaluate your situational leadership skills** to understand your dominant leadership style. A useful tool for this purpose would be the Leader Behavior Analysis II (LBAII) Scoring Test from Ken Blanchard Companies. This test will give you an indication of how flexible your style is and which leadership styles you are failing to use. Review the results and make plans for improvement.
3. **Try the model with a small group first.** Start to develop your situational leadership skills by using the model with a maximum group of three people. Make an assessment of each person. Determine the most suitable leadership style for each person in each major assignment. Start managing them with the identified styles.
4. **Expand gradually.** Once you get more comfortable with situational leadership and see positive results, expand the model gradually to the rest of the team. Keep it simple at first by initially establishing a primary leadership style for each direct report. As your level of confidence with the model increases, change the style for each major task.
5. **Avoid bypassing development levels.** With recently hired employees, some managers make the mistake of quickly shifting from the S1 directly to S3 or S4 leadership style. This usually affects performance. Always remember to apply the leadership styles in sequence through the development cycle.
6. **Follow up, check, and adjust.** In all four leadership styles, make sure to do the following:
    o   Identify desired outcomes and ensure that goals are clear.
    o   Observe and monitor performance.
    o   Give feedback to the individual.
    o   Change the leadership style as the individual moves forward or backward to another development level.
7. **Use it for self development.** Use the situational leadership model to identify your own development level and seek the direction and support that you need.

Multi Vendor Sourcing

While sticking with one vendor for a given technology solution has historically been the favored approach, the commoditization of many technologies has meant that using best of breed solution providers is becoming increasingly cost effective. Evaluate the pros and cons of taking a vendor agnostic approach to technology purchasing.

The Multi-Vendor Strategy

Vendors are now employing service oriented architectures and developing tools using open standards, such as XML and SOAP, that make a multi vendor strategy more feasible. Because of this trend, companies are free to employ best of breed systems that are specifically designed to excel in just one, or a few, applications instead of going with large, integrated, single vendor solutions. However, while multi vendor strategies do offer more tailored solutions, they still carry a variety of potential costs, including:

- Fragmented buying power due to fewer volume purchases.
- Higher testing costs, resulting from more complex integration issues.
- Duplication of technology resulting from multiple disparate packages.
- Duplicate data entry and redundant data storage due to poor integration.
- Greater human resource requirements in terms of hiring IT staff who are familiar with different hardware platforms, operating systems, databases, and programming languages.
- Reduced ability to reuse development code.
- Increased support costs for multiple integrated development environments (IDEs), which also increases the complexity involved in building backup sets and configuring server environments.

- Increased likelihood of finger pointing among vendors if there is a problem.
- Inconsistent user interface, resulting in higher training costs.
- Compromised business intelligence and knowledge management initiatives, as data is dispersed across various vendor solutions.

The Single-Vendor, Integrated Solution Strategy

While advanced functionality is sometimes compromised, large enterprise solution vendors promote their all in one product suites based on the promise of lower integration costs, strong vendor relationships, and volume discounts. Yet, sticking with a single vendor solution also comes with its own unique cost factors. Consider the following:

- Higher customization costs to bring the solution up to the standards of a best of breed solution.
- Added costs for integration of advanced functionality.
- Fewer integration benefits than you might have hoped for if your "integrated" solution was pieced together after acquiring several best of breed vendors (i.e. different hardware platforms, databases, or operating systems for various modules).
- Loss of control, as the balance of power is shifted towards the vendor (i.e. you lose the ability to walk away from a vendor).
- Loss of ability to shop around, thus over paying for the given functionality (i.e. customers often pay a premium price for leading market brands).
- Limited awareness of new technologies and products as they become available in the market.
- Increased risk of being forced to upgrade products according to the vendor's schedule, instead of based on the company's own needs.
- Total dependence on a given architecture and infrastructure.
- Reduced ability to explore more cost effective open source solutions.

- Loss of personalized service offered by smaller vendors.

Action Plan

1. **Define the business process.** Even if you are an SAP shop, SAP should not be your default solution for every business process. Determine whether the process in question is a stable, industry standard process for which the incumbent has a time tested solution (e.g. a general ledger system), or is a new, rapidly evolving, innovative one for which there is no standard solution (e.g. supply chain collaboration). In the latter case, finding a niche player might be the better option.
2. **Identify a preferred architecture.** If you plan on taking a multi vendor approach, find vendors whose solutions are compatible with your preferred architecture (consider your level of in house expertise with J2EE versus .NET, for example). Note: if you go with a single integrated vendor, this decision might already be made for you.
3. **Weigh implementation vs. customization costs.** An enterprise suite may offer superior integration, but lack the functionality available from best of breed vendors. Consider the potential cost savings and revenue gleaned from superior integration and better access to shared data versus the potential competitive advantage and cost savings gained from advanced functionality offered by a best-of-breed vendor.
4. **Centralize all IT purchasing.** You might be using a multi vendor strategy without even knowing it. Rogue IT purchasing and decentralized spending can lead to your IT department supporting vendors that you had not intended on supporting. Make sure you put an end to this activity.
5. **Centralize information and vendor management.** Even if you use multiple vendors, it is important that information and data be centrally collected, controlled, and monitored. Having a single point of contact for all internal technology support issues and all vendor communications will allow you to target recurring technical issues, improve operational efficiencies, collect data in real time, support decision-making, and improve

customer satisfaction. A central management strategy will also allow you to monitor vendor performance and ensure that different vendors are meeting service levels and warranty obligations.

6. **Choose standards based, customizable solutions.** Make sure that best of breed solutions are standards based, connect to existing applications using simple interfaces, are highly configurable to accommodate various processes, and offer the scalability and security that you require. Make sure that all new applications are fully interoperable and able to share data, in real time if necessary. This strategy will also allow you to upgrade certain parts of your overall enterprise solution (i.e. CRM, ERP) without running into conflicts that require building unnecessarily costly interfaces.

7. **Consider hardware purchases.** Extend your analysis of a multi vendor strategy to hardware purchases as well.

   o *PC Hardware:* While functional differences between devices is decreasing due to commoditization, vendor processes and product support issues still favor a single vendor approach when it comes to PC and server hardware. Supporting additional vendors can:
     ▪ Add to image preparation costs and can increase problem resolution times.
     ▪ Add more cost per month per desktop for support.
     ▪ Increase maintenance, problem detection, and problem resolution times.

   o *Storage:* Buying storage technology from a single vendor could end up costing you considerably more per megabyte than sourcing from multiple vendors. Also, because storage is largely a commodity purchase, large vendors, recognizing the lower potential for revenue, often look to sell software packages (which you may or may not need) just to get the hardware sale.

In Summary
While picking up a new best of breed application may seem like a simple decision, it could end up costing you more than you think. Make sure you consider all of the costs involved before inadvertently jumping into a multi-vendor strategy.

Need a Career Boost? Try Financial Techniques

Sound IT investment decisions cannot be made without using the right financial measures. Integrate these techniques into the decision-making process to maximize IT's alignment with the business and broaden your career opportunities.

The Right Tool for the Job

In various research we discover that in most mid-sized enterprises, IT and business are poorly aligned. As a result, a majority of IT projects are not meeting the full satisfaction of business leaders. The research also shows that only 26% of mid-sized enterprises use financial measures like ROI to assist in making project decisions. Organizations using these measures are more aligned with the business and achieve higher project success rates.

The Time Value of Money

The simplest explanation of the time value of money is that a dollar today is worth more than a dollar in the future. This is due to compound interest. Interest is used to compensate people for certain risks and to cause people to want to save or invest rather than spend the money today. Calculating the time value of money is critical when evaluating a project that takes two to three years to recover its cost. NPV, IRR, and EVA are financial measures based on the time value of money. IT departments that incorporate a variety of financial measures into their decision-making process achieve optimal success. Recognizing that there is no silver bullet, they understand the trade-offs of each. Below is a brief description of the traditional financial measures used by these organizations to improve their investment decisions.

Calculating the time value of money is critical when evaluating a

- **Return on Investment (ROI):** ROI is the most popular, and least understood, financial tool. Since it is a generic tool that has taken on numerous forms (return on invested capital, return on assets, and return on equity, just to name a few). Although ROI can be applied in a number of different ways, the underlying formula is the same: (gains - investment costs)/investment costs. ROI is expressed as a percentage. The higher the percentage, the more attractive the investment. For an ROI evaluation to be effective, the projects being compared require similar underlying parameters or variables.

- **Payback Period:** This calculation estimates how long it takes a project to cover its initial costs (i.e. break-even point). Payback period is the easiest tool to use because it only examines the initial cost to be recovered, and rarely takes the time value of money into consideration when calculating future returns. For small, simple IT investments with short paybacks and highly predictable returns, this is a useful tool for prioritizing projects.

- **Net Present Value (NPV):** Unlike payback period, it translates a project's future cash flows into a present value. This involves developing a single NPV using a discount rate that progressively reduces the values of cash flows the further in the future they occur. The major limitations of NPV are that it relies on a long period for cash flows and maintains a static view of the future. Decision makers must take care not to blindly sacrifice lower-value, short-term options with quick payback for higher-value projects with long-term payback.

- **Internal Rate of Return (IRR):** The IRR on an investment is the required return that results in a zero NPV when it is used as the discount rate. Unfortunately, the only way to find the IRR is by trial and error. When using IRR, a higher yield is better, and provides the basis for project ranking. In order for a project to warrant consideration, its return rate must be above a predetermined hurdle rate, the lowest being the rate required to cover the initial cost. Like NPV, IRR also fails to address the strategic impact of the return. A project with a low IRR, but significant strategic implications, may be passed over in favor of a small-value project with a high IRR.

- **Economic Value Added (EVA):** This tool uses the discounted cash flow technique, but takes an important step beyond the tools above by attempting to quantify a project's impact on the enterprise's overall health. This is a method used by financial analysts to estimate the current and future viability of a company. Although calculating a project's EVA involves a lot of math, the basic concept is simple: measuring the incremental value created by an investment.

Recommendations

1. **IT organizations must work with the business to improve the application of these traditional financial tools.** Understanding when and why to use a financial tool is not an overnight revelation. IT, finance, and business leaders must work closely to develop a consistent decision-making approach for different IT investments. By working together, IT will improve its decision-making abilities and increase project performance. Meanwhile, business leaders will improve their understanding of IT and how to define its value.
2. **Perform ongoing calculations to develop decision-making ability.** Performing payback, ROI, NPV, IRR, and EVA calculations is an ongoing process. Most organizations feel that a one-time calculation is sufficient, but this is not true. Once a project is given the green light, organizations rarely monitor the calculation. Revisiting and tuning these calculations throughout a project's lifecycle is essential to improving the application of these tools.
3. **Standardize measuring processes across your organization.** If people in different departments are using different metrics to measure project performance, you will have difficulty comparing figures and business cases, and setting benchmarks. Make sure IT's measurement tools are comparing "apples to apples" - do not assume that because someone is using the same acronym, their methodology is the same.

In Summary

IT managers making investment decisions without relying on proven financial techniques and management are doing so at their own peril. Take financial courses to hone this critical skill.

No Business Strategy IT Planning

Aligning IT with the business should be a significant management priority for all IT decision-makers. The problem is that many small- to mid-sized enterprises (SMEs) do not have a formalized business strategy for IT to align with. Interview business leaders to facilitate the IT planning process and align IT's project plans with business goals.

The Price of Poor Alignment

The purpose of IT is to deliver an infrastructure that allows the business to attain its strategic goals. In order to do this, the business must play a key role in defining the kinds of IT projects that can help drive the business. Meanwhile, IT must be able to inform the business on the feasibility of projects given its budget constraints.

Unfortunately for most mid-sized enterprises, there is a disconnect between the two groups. Senior management does not understand why some IT projects do not fulfill expectations. Meanwhile, IT complains about unrealistic time frames, lack of staff, and poorly defined project scope. Failure to meet business expectations even once can severely tarnish IT's reputation.

Bridge the Gap with a "Wants and Needs" List

IT strategy mapped onto a solid business plan increases alignment, decreases the risk of project failure, and encourages proactive investment decisions.

Luckily, a clearly documented business strategy is not a necessary blueprint to develop an IT strategy. A SME can create a high-impact IT strategy simply by asking business leaders how IT can help them attain their goals. IT instantly raises its profile from a cost center to strategic enabler, gains critical insight into key business processes, and helps business leaders understand how IT can deliver strategic value.

Recommendations

1. **Work with the CEO to establish an IT steering committee.** Outline the key benefits of engaging business leaders in the IT planning process. Volunteer to facilitate these discussions emphasizing the end goal: creating a list of IT projects that will help the CEO's business leaders reach their goals. Emphasize the necessity of creating a planning group to objectively evaluate the IT project list. The CEO, the head of IT, and business leaders representing each business unit should be on this committee. The mandate of the committee is twofold:
   o   To choose a list of IT projects on an annual basis.
   o   To review IT's progress on a quarterly basis.
2. **Interview each business leader and obtain a list of key IT projects.** Presumably, the people being interviewed are also on the IT steering committee. If this is not the case, communicate the role that the interview plays in the IT planning process. Ask each business leader how IT can help the unit reach its strategic goals. Instruct them to write a list of key IT projects that will help them reach their strategic goals. It is the business leaders' responsibility to justify the business case for each project request.
3. **Prioritize projects.** Gather all IT projects into a master project list and identify synergies and dependencies. Put all the projects into a timeline and allocate the necessary resources, listing any new skill requirements. Do not underestimate the power of this tool. It illustrates how project scope, time, and budget are interconnected, and helps IT manage business expectations.
4. **Present a tactical plan.** Present the master project list to the IT steering committee, highlighting synergies, dependencies, and resource requirements. The IT decision-maker must embrace the role of master project manager. In the end, it is IT's responsibility to present feasibility and manage expectations. Work with business leaders to select the IT projects that are best for the overall health of the company.

In Summary

The lack of a formal business strategy does not mean that IT cannot create a plan aligned with business goals and objectives. Facilitate IT planning by asking business leaders how the department can help them attain their strategic goals.

Office Politics

If office politics is a term that leaves a bad taste in your mouth, you better buck up and change your attitude. Political skills such as managing relationships, communicating effectively, and identifying stakeholders are all critical for IT leaders. Make sure that you have a firm grasp on the skills and tasks necessary to ensure your success in dealing with office politics.

Action Plan

Politics begin when there are more than two people working together. It happens in families, nonprofits, small businesses, government agencies, and especially the corporate world. Here are some techniques that will help you deal with office politics and prevent it from spinning out of control:

1. **Consider your work ethic.** Before you do anything else, you must get yourself prepared to handle the political battle that lies ahead. Consider the following:
   - Win credibility by having a personal standard of excellence in all that you say and do.
   - Build a great reputation by constantly striving to achieve the results you want and being successful with your projects.
   - Be aware of dysfunctional business environments and people who have unhealthy intentions.
2. **React accordingly.** Not only do you have to prepare yourself, you also need to make sure that your behavior doesn't encourage harmful office politics. Here are a few actions to think about:
   - Facilitate shifting the blame from "who" to "what" when things go wrong.
   - Make sure you attend social work functions with your staff; otherwise, be accused of not being a team player. Remember, these are still work events.
   - Never put in writing what you wouldn't say to someone's face.
   - Do not use e-mail when attempting to solve a conflict.

- o   Don't get caught up in someone else's battle. It is to your advantage to stay neutral.
- o   Use the grapevine to keep abreast of what is going on in the company.
- o   Refrain from criticizing coworkers and staff behind their backs, lest you end up with unnecessary enemies if word gets back to them.
3. **Know whom you're dealing with.** Figure out who the key people are in your organization and consider their goals, perspectives, motives, and their relationships with IT and others in the organization. Get to know the decision-makers, influential supporters, and opponents. Once you have built these relationships, they can help you get through politically driven situations. For example, strong relationships will be helpful when seeking approval for a budget or project, and will improve dealings with senior management in general.
4. **Engage customers and users in continuous communication.** Good communication is the most critical factor in dealing with office politics. Focus on developing communication skills to do the following:
- o   Form solid communication pathways with your users to keep them updated on the status of pertinent projects and problems.
- o   Avert the counterproductive, spirit crushing, time consuming detrimental effects of office gossip by keeping all lines of communication open between the IT department and the rest of the organization.
- o   Draw key customers, both internal and external, into the IT governance process by asking each to select from a list of projects their most important initiatives for the upcoming year.
5. **Make a friend in every department.** Building and maintaining relationships with opponents and allies throughout the organization is imperative. To be successful with office politics, you must be a good listener and facilitator, and pay attention to what is spoken and unspoken.
- o   Form alliances and bring them into the decision-making process. This will enable you to seek endorsements from early adopters by communicating the benefits of a new system and demonstrating its value.

o Solve sticky political situations by leveraging relationships that have been built outside the context of individual situations.
o Learn some of the unwritten company rules by cultivating alliances and mentors in high places.
6. **Be ready for political change.** Battle the ever changing political office environment by understanding what the drivers are within your organization, what the goals are of the different stakeholders, and the nature of existing relationships. This will help you stay ahead of political shifts, which will frequently occur. At the same time, keep your own strategy clearly in mind. When political changes occur, you need to know how to make judgments that won't compromise your credibility. Expect the unexpected and plan mitigation strategies.
7. **Be patient.** Being a person in management, you are a change agent, and patience is necessary when pressing for your initiatives. Sustainable change needs to take place over time. Take a long term view to help keep progress with change initiatives in perspective.
8. **Don't put up with gossip.** Take charge and keep gossip under control. Gossip is the engine driving negative office politics. Your staff relies on you to clear obstacles that prevent them from completing their work in a timely and effective manner. If coworkers or peers are dabbling in office gossip, then call them on it - preferably in private. Don't be afraid to pull new employees under your wing if you feel that they are being influenced by gossipers.

In Summary

Career success is not just about IT knowledge and talent. If you want your career to prosper, gain allies, work to build credibility, stay visible, and stifle harmful gossip to become a politically savvy IT leader.

Penetration Testing

Making the case for penetration testing is as complicated and necessary as making the case for any type of security investment. Use the following advice to help you develop your business case for penetration testing.

What Exactly Is a Penetration Test?

Not to be confused with a vulnerability scan, a penetration test is a systematic process that attempts to locate known vulnerabilities in applications, networks, operating systems, and even policies and procedures, in order to gain access to systems. Penetration testing is an increasingly important component of holistic risk management.

Action Plan

Use the following tips to help you assess the benefits and costs of penetration testing, as well as streamline acceptance by senior management.

1. **Valuate your assets.** If you want to make the case for running a penetration test on a particular database, for example, you'll need to figure out how much that database is worth to the business and what it would cost the company if it were lost or compromised.
    o   No asset is an island - nearly all technologies are interdependent. To help make your case, be prepared to show the domino effect that the compromise of one system will have and how one can be used to launch an attack on another. This will help senior management view penetration testing more holistically and see that each component is critical to the success of the entire system.
2. **Don't base your argument solely on the fear factor.** If you don't perform penetration testing, you won't know where your weak spots are, and it's just a question of time before a malicious force takes you down. Okay, so how will penetration testing directly increase revenue or cut costs? Your case must address these business issues as well.

○ Most well-executed technology implementations will be accompanied by some type of return on investment calculation (ROI), such as a Payback Period, Net Present Value (NPV), or Internal Rate of Return (IRR). Find these numbers, and assess what kind of impact there would be on these figures if the technology implementation were compromised.

3. **Calculate the total cost of penetration testing.** Penetration testing isn't free you'll need to make a total cost calculation. This calculation includes not only the direct costs of performing the test, but also the costs of any fixes you'll need to apply if a vulnerability is detected. In the final analysis, how much you're willing to spend on fixes will be a factor of the value of the asset to the business. The goal is for the total cost of penetration testing to be less than the benefits gained by performing the test and protecting the business from the loss of that asset.

4. **Calculate the risk of the test itself.** The penetration test itself could put your organization at risk. The two major risks to consider are that a third-party penetration tester could gain access to sensitive systems or data, or the tests themselves could cause a system outage or data loss. Conduct a risk analysis of the penetration test itself and decide how much risk your organization is willing to carry. You may decide to mitigate risks by placing limits on network access and stopping tests once they've reached certain thresholds.

5. **Piggyback a revenue generating project.** One of the goals of all technology implementations should be deployment of a secure system. A revenue generating project, such as an e-commerce Web site, provides a perfect opportunity to work in penetration testing as a project milestone since it will directly help in achieving the risk and security management goals of the project. Watch for such an opportunity, and take advantage of it to prove the value of penetration testing.

6. **Plan the scope and depth of testing.** When it comes to penetration testing, you get what you pay for. How many systems you want to test and how deeply you want to test them will have a direct impact on the total cost of

penetration testing. This is ultimately your call, but you may opt to be selective in your testing to keep costs low.

7. **Consider timesaving options.** Giving the penetration tester information like a firewall Access Control List (ACL) or network map could save time. While this step seems to contradict the idea that the tester should only have what the hacker has, it can make for more targeted and accurate testing, as well as reduce costs. It's more and more common for businesses to give third-party penetration testers partial information to help them plan and execute tests, so don't feel like you're cheating.

In Summary

Making a sound business case for a seemingly "no brainer" security investment like penetration testing is harder than it looks. But at a time when you must prove the business value of every IT investment in quantitative terms, you have to make the effort or else risk being denied.

Play Nice with Auditors

As far as Sarbanes-Oxley audits are concerned, there's no argument. You *simply have to do it,* or else risk litigation, damage to company reputation, and a host of other unsavory problems. When the auditor does show up, avoid making enemies. Use cooperation, tact, and a little insider knowledge to help facilitate the rather unlikable auditing process.

Action Plan

Below are a few tips for dealing with auditors. While they won't make you feel warm and fuzzy about being audited, they will - if followed - help ease the pain and make the process go more smoothly for all parties involved.

1. **Practice smiling. Really.** Politeness calls for lots of smiling, even if you're clenching and grinding your teeth behind that smile. Obstinacy, rudeness, or a reluctance to answer questions will only make the auditor's time at your company stretch out far longer than is necessary.
2. **Ask nothing.** As tempting as it may be to question the auditor about his or her findings, recommendations, and so on, remember one simple rule: *don't do it.* SarbOx regulations expressly forbid communications of this kind between auditors and CIOs. For example, auditors:
    o   Cannot make recommendations to CIOs for the best way to assess and document IT controls, as this qualifies as a conflict of interest.
    o   Cannot be the ones to actually help enterprises become compliant, even though they are likely the most qualified people to do so.
    o   Must record any conversations with CIOs. Why? The very fact that a CIO asks a question demonstrates a potential deficiency that the auditor must now test!
3. **Understand that auditors are in the dark as well.** The Public Company Accounting Oversight Board - http://www.pcaobus.org - (PCAOB) governs the entire SarbOx auditing process. And yet, the PCAOB has not given auditors any methodology whatsoever for auditing and documenting IT controls. When auditors do show up at your door, try to bear in mind that the reason for their unrelenting thoroughness is

rooted in the fact that they are just covering their own bases (as you should also do).
- o It doesn't look as though auditor confusion will end any time soon, as the PCAOB still refuses to recommend or endorse any single IT controls standard or testing method.
- o Current public opinion, however, seems to be leaning toward - http://www.isaca.org/cobit.htm - (COBIT) as the closest thing to a cure-all for SarbOx compliance woes.
4. **Have your documentation ready.** Auditors love to see documented IT controls, so the more paperwork you have on this subject, the less time the auditor will have to spend on it. Conducting in-house audits prior to the auditor's arrival is time-consuming, but ultimately worth the effort.
5. **Tell the truth.** Cooperate with the auditor - it is simply the smartest and best thing to do. Clouding the issue by telling half-truths or omitting important details is only going to land you in hot water. If there is an insecurity in one of your processes or IT controls, the auditor is going to find it anyway. It will look far worse on the auditors' report if they record finding a vulnerability that you flat-out denied than one that you were upfront about in the first place.
6. **Share your expertise with the auditor.** When asked, be sure to explain how, why, and by what method your enterprise has assessed and mitigated risk. Actually demonstrate in writing how you've done it. Many SarbOx auditors are new to this game, so it's up to you to display a willingness to impart all aspects of the company's decision-making process as it relates to security. This is especially important when dealing with auditors whose experience lies in auditing financial controls rather than IT controls.
7. **Remember that size doesn't matter to an auditor.** PCAOB guidelines do not account for company size. There is no "lite" version for Sarbanes-Oxley audits, and SMBs are expected to adhere to the same SarbOx requirements as Fortune 500 enterprises. Consequently, auditors aren't going to cut you slack simply because yours is a smaller company with limited resources.

In Summary

No one enjoys being audited, but don't allow the auditor-auditee relationship become an adversarial one. Practice diplomacy, restraint, and a generous dose of patience.

Process Development Needs BPII

Process refinement is one term that gets lost in the shuffle as organizations focus on two types of BPM solutions: Business Process Modeling/Analysis (BPM/A) tools and Business Process Management (BPM) suites. Understand how a Business Process Improvement Initiative (BPII) drives process refinement and the roles BPM solutions play in BPII to avoid spending money on software that simply goes down the drain of negative ROI.

The Process Refinement Trinity

A business process represents the work, people, systems, and business partners that perform in the enterprise to provide a product or service to their customers. Process refinement focuses on making components within an enterprise work more efficiently and effectively. Although IT and business leaders typically see process refinement as a single entity, it actually involves three separate but related activities:

1. **Process analysis** identifies, assesses and documents existing processes in the enterprise.
2. **Process management** implements, automates and monitors the processes discovered through process analysis.
3. **Business Process Improvement Initiative (BPII).** Organizations can perform process analysis and management separately. The best approach, however, is to perform these activities within a narrow business context. A BPII is a business-driven project with the aim of focusing on and optimizing processes – automated and manual – that provide the greatest immediate value to the enterprise.

...Paved with Good Intentions

Companies that start on the road to process refinement typically stumble over two problems:

1. **Determining the right way to implement each activity.** This typically involves determining whether the enterprise should use software tools which triggers a number of questions:
   o If tools are to be used, then what kinds of tools are best?
   o For which activity should tools be used?
   o How sophisticated should these tools be?
   o What level of integration should these tools have with each other?
   o What are the costs of these tools and how does that affect ROI?
2. **Finding the right mix of these three activities.** Leaders tasked with process refinement typically attempt to address the questions above using a top-down approach. This invariably leads to the view that the three refinement activities are subsets of each other. It also implies that to meet the goals of process refinement, business and IT leaders should implement BPM tools that come with a BPM/A toolset.

This model presents the three approaches to process refinement that most enterprises tend to follow, with the arrows showing how to move from each approach towards BPN.

- **Process refinement as a pure business-focused initiative** with no automation and no interaction with IT. This occurs in mature organizations that see IT as a cost center instead of as a business enabler. These organizations have very mature, well-documented, manual, paper-based processes with no automated management or refinement strategies. There can be real benefit found here by honing the discipline of changing/eliminating how work is done – and by whom – without using automation. This approach to process refinement, however, delivers a fraction of the value that would be possible if some automation and tools were incorporated into the BPII.
- **Process refinement as an IT-focused initiative with indirect business value** due to the use of BPM/A tools. Companies that fall into this type of process refinement usually have strong business/IT relationships and

recognize the importance of process modeling and documentation. The companies start with BPM/A tools as part of a Service-Oriented Architecture (SOA) or process integration initiative instead as part of an overarching BPII. The organization as a whole will see benefit due to reduced cost from the reusable components and processes discovered, and because the software development and procurement becomes more tightly aligned to business processes.

- **Process refinement as an IT-focused initiative with minimal business value** due to the use of BPM suites outside of a business context. This is an undesirable option because it is the most expensive and delivers the least value to the organization. Businesses that direct IT to purchase a BPM suite thinking that it will "make their process better" will not realize any benefit until the company changes the way its people, processes, and tools function. Any immediate benefits that the organization realizes will quickly diminish due to the difficulty in integrating and automating the other poorly managed and documented processes.

Recommendations

1. **Business-focused companies should add automation and tools to the mix.** Companies with a business-focused process refinement strategy should start looking to automation and modeling tools to increase the value of the BPII. Bring IT on board to help develop a strategy for incorporating technology into the BPII.
2. **Enterprises using BPM/A should develop a BPII.** Although BPM/A tools are invaluable in documenting and designing processes, they cannot replace a formal BPII. Companies using BPM/A tools should develop their BPII before designing and deploying any new processes. Doing this will reduce the process design effort because the BPII essentially serves as a best practices guide for process design and deployment.
3. **Enterprises with a BPM suite and no BPII should focus their efforts on BPM/A.** Organizations that have purchased a BPM suite should leverage the BPM/A

capabilities available in the suite to help them drive more value from their acquisition. Modeling/analyzing other processes within the organization beyond the initial processes will ensure the investment in a BPM suite continues to deliver value.

4. **Make the BPM suite the last item on the list.** To avoid succumbing to vendor pressure and false promises, only buy a BPM suite when it is necessary. Focus on developing the BPII documentation and then modeling the processes in the organization. Identify all high-value processes that IT can automate, and then buy the appropriate BPM engine that fulfills the needs of the enterprise.

In Summary

Process refinement is a huge undertaking that requires more than modeling tools and tightly integrated management suites. Look beyond BPM technology. Focus instead on developing a BPII that will drive process refinement and help stop the company from sending money down the drain of negative ROI.

Professional Services Keys to Success

Practice leaders of professional services firms understand that success involves a balancing act: building an experienced and talented team, sustaining trusted relationships with clients, performing engagements that deliver client value, and operating a profitable business. Measuring the factors of a flourishing practice is critical to maintaining this balance. Start with seven metrics for successful practice management.

Build Business

1. **Return on Invested Time** (Effective Business Development)

Whether a sole practitioner or partner in a larger firm, success is measured by the business generated for the firm. Time, as they say, is money. There are many aspects of business development: publishing, marketing, speaking, and responding to client requests for proposals. The key is optimizing business development time to generate revenue.

ROIT = Engagement Revenue / Opportunity Business Development Hours

Most professional firms set revenue targets for the business developers, often the senior partners, in the firm. As a business developer, there are always opportunities to explore, projects to chase; it is easy to become distracted and fall behind revenue goals. For example, a business developer that needs to drive $100,000 every month will focus relentlessly on those activities that get him or her closer to that objective. An opportunity that will take a week to pursue, propose and close, better help him or her attain at least 25% ($25,000) of the monthly target.

Of course, ROIT should not be the sole metric used to assess the performance of business developers; sales need to be profitable for the organization. Combine ROIT with one or more of the additional metrics outlined below.

2. Win Ratio

Related to ROIT is the frequency with which opportunities are converted into revenue producing engagements, that is, how often the firm wins business.

Win Ratio = Number of Wins / Number of Proposals

A low Win Ratio is a potential indication of three different business issues: a business developer pursuing too many low percentage opportunities, proposal quality is consistently falling below that of the competition or proposal price is consistently falling outside client expectations. For example a business developer with a low win ratio of 25% needs to identify, pursue and propose four times to expect a single win. Using the example above, if that business developer needs to generate $100,000 each month, s/he needs to pursue four opportunities worth at least $100,000 each to meet expectations.

Deliver Value

3. Customer Satisfaction

Providing a professional service is all about relationships – the relationship you have with your clients, the relationships your client has with your prospective clients. Having happy clients is critical to the firm's reputation, to repeat business and to new business.

There are two aspects of customer satisfaction, both of which require a simple survey to assess.

Engagement Satisfaction – Conducted at the conclusion of every project, a short survey allows the client to comment on the services provided. Sample questions can include:

- How well were client needs and expectations met on this project?

- Was the value delivered significantly greater than fees paid?

  Relationship Satisfaction – Conducted annually, this survey tests the culmination of all projects performed for a client. Sample questions can include:

- How well does the firm provide a consistently high level of quality services?
- How easy is the firm to do business with?
- Would the client recommend the firm to other organizations?

4. **Client Retention**

A more tangible indication of client satisfaction is repeat business. Does the client come to the firm for services year after year?

Client Retention =
Clients w/2 Yr Pay History / # of Paying Clients Last Year

The cost of winning a new client can be substantially higher than winning new business with existing clients. For this reason, it is important to understand how well the firm drives repeat business with existing clients year over year.

Operate Profitably

5. **Days Sales Outstanding**

To remain viable, any business needs timely cash flow. For a professional service firm, getting clients to pay bills is essential to meet payroll and to fund business development. Days Sales Outstanding (DSO) is a measure of the number of days it takes a firm to collect revenues billed.

DSO = Accounts Receivable / Total Revenue in Period x Days in Period

For example, many firms bill fees earned on a monthly basis. To maintain a healthy cash flow, a firm needs to consistently collect billings within a time equivalent to their billing cycle. For example, a firm that generates $200,000 in revenue during a given month and is owed $200,000 in billed fees has a DSO of 30 days ((200,000/200,000) x 30 days). A firm with a DSO below the days in its billing cycle is receiving prompt payment and thereby strong cash flow. A firm with a DSO greater than billing cycle risks falling behind in collections and runs a greater risk of not getting paid.

6. Utilization

A firm's professional staff is its greatest asset and, for most companies, its single largest source of operating costs. Keeping staff working on billable engagements is critical to optimize returns.

Utilization = Total Billable Hours / Total Available Hours

In this equation, total available hours include all time for which an employee is paid by the firm: billable, business development, professional development, administration, sick days and vacation.

Target utilization will differ by professional in the firm. While utilization levels vary from firm to firm, Principals who have business development responsibility typically have a target utilization of 50% or below. Junior staffers, who have very little business development responsibility, typically are expected to have a high utilization of 90% or more. Set a utilization target and monitor it for each employee. Where utilization for an individual consistently falls below the target, action may be needed to bolster the billability of that professional. If utilization as a whole is low, this may point to an overly optimistic sales plan or overly abundant staffing pool.

7. **Profitability**

In the end, running a business is all about profitable cash flow. Profits from operations permit an organization to make investments back into the business- to strengthen the team, to drive business development activities, and to raise the profile of the company. There are several ways to measure profitability:

Gross Margin = Gross Profit / Total Revenue

where Gross Profit = Total Revenue – Cost of Operations (Staff, Facilities, Business Development)

Client Margin = Gross Profit of the Client / Total Revenue of the Client

where Gross Profit for the Client = Total Revenue for the Client – Cost to Serve that Client (Staff, Facilities, Business Development)

Margin Per Billable Hour = Gross Profit / Billable Hours

While every firm will measure gross margin as part of its standard financial reporting, this metric is less effective when it comes to identifying potential areas of improvement.

For instance, client margin is a good way to measure variability in profitability across different clients. It helps a firm determine which companies in its portfolio could be considered "best" clients, and to identify companies who seem to consume a great deal of non-billable resources for limited return.

Margin per billable hour is a useful tool to test billing rates. While many factors go into setting a billing rate, such as compensation, non-billable expenses, utilization, collections and competition, margin per billable hour allows the firm to understand how costs of running its business are covered by billable work.

Key Takeaways

1. **Focus on a few vital metrics.** It can be easy to become distracted with the many aspects of running a successful business. IT Leaders should encourage business executives to keep the number of performance measures limited to a select few, such as the seven included here.
2. **Maintain balance.** No single metric is a true indicator of overall success. Achieving a high level of utilization does not guarantee profitable operations. Work with business executives to select at least one metric from each of the categories, Build, Deliver and Operate, to get a balanced view.
3. **Understand drivers.** Having insight into firm performance is only the first step. Knowing what to do when a metric falls below target comes next. Work with business executives to diagnose which business factors can affect each metric to determine potential actions that can improve performance.
4. **Develop a repeatable metric reporting process.** Whether using a Business Intelligence product, a project accounting system or manual processes, breakdown each metric into the specific data needs, determine how to source and collect the data and to consistently report on the key metrics.

In Summary

Professional Services is a people and relationship business. Clients value the advice and experience of staff but they buy based on trust and credibility of the firm. IT leaders should anticipate how executives intend to monitor company performance by understanding seven key metrics and the data required to support them.

Project Portfolio Optimization

You have decided that managing your IT projects using a portfolio approach is the way to go. To get the most out of this approach, a system of ongoing project analysis is a must. Maximize the returns on your portfolio by actively managing your IT projects.

Optimizing a Portfolio

When an organization commits to a project, an allotment of money, labor, and resources is invested. While some of these investments are substantial, many organizations remain passive investors in the project. They often leave the success, failure, and return on their project investments to chance. IT departments should actively manage their portfolios to maximize returns on their investments. With the proper analysis, they can identify, evaluate, and rank their projects like investment opportunities. As a result, resources can be directed to the highest-payback projects and culled from marginal ones. The three traditional approaches to analyzing project value are as follows:

1. **Mathematical programming.** Focuses on maximizing value, but does not take strategic alignment or portfolio balance into consideration.
2. **Classical.** Maximizes the value of a portfolio through either financial or non-financial scoring, sorting models, or checklists. This technique has been criticized for relying on financial information and not finding an optimal project mix.
3. **Mapping.** Displays the links between various projects and strategic alignment, but does not consider the balance of the portfolio or how to maximize its financial return.

A Well-Balanced Approach to Project Analysis

To provide a complete picture of a portfolio's current and future viability, your analysis must include a hybrid of the three traditional techniques by looking at:

1. **Alignment.** Measures support for the organization's business strategies and specific objectives.
2. **Achievability.** Measures your capacity to execute and complete the projects.
3. **Value.** Measures the expected benefits and rate of return of the portfolio.
4. **Balance.** Measures how the project portfolio is balancing risk and reward.

Recommendations

1. **Measure your projects' alignment.** Before you can analyze a project portfolio, it is critical to list your organization's business strategies in priority sequence. The value of a project cannot be properly assessed without understanding how it maps onto the strategic plan. Assessing a project's strategic alignment is a qualitative measurement.
2. **Look at project achievability.** In order to complete the projects in your portfolio, you must have the necessary time, resource capacity, and budget. To properly evaluate achievability, create a project list, an inventory of resources, their current allocation, and estimated costs. Do not overlook the impact of project interdependencies. By properly quantifying your project interdependencies, portfolio performance can be improved in the following four ways:

   o **Refine the order and timing of your projects.** Lower the organization's overall execution costs, avoid duplication, re-use deliverables, and capitalize on project synergies.
   o **Develop a sourcing strategy for your projects.** Avoid squandered resources by basing your resource allocation on the needs of the portfolio as a whole.
   o **Resolve conflicts between projects.** Get the "big picture" perspective needed to ensure that projects with conflicting goals are not selected.
   o **Dispatch projects that do not fit the profile.** Recognize projects that are not improving the overall return on the portfolio.
   o **Select the models to measure the value of your IT projects.** While financial modeling is a necessity for

measuring value, it is not the only aspect of value. It is imperative to select models that allow you to compare one project to another.

- o For financial modeling, consider the following models: Net Present Value (NPV), Internal Rate of Return (IRR), Expected Commercial Value (ECV), and Economic Value Added (EVA).
- o Non-financial benefits like improved customer satisfaction, increased market share, and defect reduction can also be quantified and measured.

3. **Measure the balance of your portfolio.** The goal here is find out how your portfolio is balancing risk and value. Embrace risk analysis to manage the portfolio effectively. Focusing solely on individual project value brings only one half of the business equation to the table.

- o Choose a group of projects that will generate the highest rate of return with an acceptable degree of risk.
- o On the surface, high-value projects will be the most appealing. However, if the associated risks are also high, they may not be as attractive an investment. A conservative project with limited risks may provide a limited return, and thus, undermine your organization's future viability.
- The bubble chart is an effective tool for measuring the balance of value and risk. This is due to its ability to graphically represent multiple dimensions (x-axis and y-axis). For information on bubble charts visit the following link.

http://www.computerdictionary.info/computer-term-details/Bubble-Chart

In Summary

Maximizing the return on your IT investment portfolio demands active project analysis. Use a balanced analytical approach that measures alignment, achievability, value, and the balance between risk and reward.

Projects with no Tangible Benefits

Gaining project approval usually starts with a well crafted business case that outlines how a particular solution or strategy can make or save money for an organization. The rub comes, however, when you are faced with the task of selling a project that produces only intangible benefits. Learn some strategies for selling this kind of project.

The Trouble with Intangible Benefits

It's widely accepted that the key to project approval is the coveted Business Case, in which options are outlined, benefits are quantified, and return on investment (ROI) is calculated. In most cases this approach is both efficient and effective. In cases where a tangible benefit cannot be calculated, however, the business case can be a frustrating exercise. Projects that are based on business need, but lack easily quantifiable benefits, include:

- Legal or regulatory compliance projects.
- Projects that help the organization maintain a competitive advantage.
- Infrastructure projects (i.e. to maintain or improve network performance).
- Projects that focus on increasing customer satisfaction.
- Projects that focus on increasing employee satisfaction.
- Projects that link IT initiatives to business strategies.

All of these projects can result in real benefits, but are not easily converted into an ROI calculation. There are opportunities for creatively calculating the value of intangible benefits.

Creating a Business Case without ROI

No one would argue that projects such as those listed above are not important to an enterprise, especially if you can make a case for how they align with strategic business initiatives. The key is to make a case that focuses on how

125

your project will solve a serious business problem. Your business case needs to answer two questions:

- Should we do this project?
- What is the most efficient and effective way to get it done?

The answers to these questions will form the basis of your business case. A traditional business case template may not be necessary, as you will lack much of the financial information that would normally accompany such a document. Despite your inability to quantify benefits, you must present costs and consequences of your proposal so that your audience can make an informed decision on the best course of action, should they decide to pursue the project.

Action Plan

1. **Present the problem.** Describe the current state of affairs of the enterprise, including any necessary background information pertinent to your discussion. Outline the problem the enterprise is facing. Remember who your audience is, and describe the problem in business terms, not technology terms, where possible.
2. **Describe the impact of the problem.** Describe in business terms the impact of the problem. This is different than describing the consequences of the problem. Here you want to outline how pervasive the problem is within the enterprise. For instance, if you are discussing a regulatory compliance problem, describe the systems, departments, or personnel affected in becoming compliant.
3. **Describe what will happen if the problem is not solved.** Describe the bad things that will happen if the problem is not resolved. Base your claims on reality, and specify in detail any costs that are associated. In the example above, you would discuss in real terms the consequences of not becoming compliant, such as fines, jail time, or business shutdown. Where possible, discuss real numbers.
4. **Describe the options available to solve the problem.** In this section, you present all viable alternatives available to the organization, not just the solution you hope will be

chosen. One option may be to do nothing. Wherever possible, focus on the strategic fit of the project to business goals and objectives.

5. **Quantify the costs and outline the most likely benefits of each option.** For each option presented, describe the worst and best case scenario outcomes. While you may be unable to accurately calculate benefits, you must be able to outline the costs of each option.

6. **End with a conclusion and recommendations.** This is the time to really sell your case. Outline your recommended choice of action. Describe why your recommended choice is the best one using real costs and benefits. End your case with a call to action. For example, Solution 1 must be implemented within six months to meet the regulatory compliance deadline outlined in this business case.

In Summary

Just because you cannot quantify project benefits in real numbers doesn't mean that a project is not worth pursuing. Concentrate on how your project will resolve a pressing business issue to maximize the chances of approval.

Recommendations to Protect IT Budgets

1. **Align today's budget to strategy.** A long-term strategy provides a context for today's expenditures. A three-year strategy can effectively demonstrate why developing "A" today is necessary to implementing "Z" in three years. For example, investing in the network now may be critical in the corporate strategy for implementing Unified Communications at a future date.

2. **Perform a budget review.** Arrange an annual or project-by-project budget review meeting to show how the allocated money has been spent. This demonstrates the department's spending habits and gives an opportunity to justify unexpected factors that affected the budget, such as changes in price or technology. Explain what worked out as planned, what didn't, and why.

3. **Separate "need to have" from "nice to have."** Know the difference between essential investments and those that are merely helpful. Business driven investments should already have this distinction. IT should make this difference clear in the budget for IT driven projects – actually label each line item as either essential or non-essential. Spell out the risks and consequences of not having essential items.

4. **Create budget sub-sections.** Separate the budget into projects (investments in new functions or infrastructure), and operational (day-to-day maintenance expenses). In lean times, evaluate investments based on business value returned. For operational expenses, look for ways to improve efficiency to reduce cost.

5. **Use a sharp pencil.** Research purchase costs for each line item carefully. Use current market values and look for lower-cost alternatives. Establish a vendor management program at the organization to develop a mutually beneficial client/vendor relationship. Negotiate preferable terms and prices with vendors. Using proven negotiation tactics to receive best prices will make many IT leaders look like the very essence of thrift.

6. **Get line-of-business support.** Encourage line-of-business managers to vocally push for items in the IT department's budget. Senior management loves an IT

budget that supports business priorities (i.e. bolstering the bottom line or increasing competitiveness).

7. **Be credible.** Past performance on designing and adhering to budgets will go a long way toward easing the approval process this time around.

- o Don't be overly optimistic in the projections – most companies simply can't swallow cost overruns in the midst of a recession or downturn. Be realistic.
- o Be complete in the itemization – don't forget maintenance and consulting.
- o Triple-check the figures. Erroneous numbers will paint an amateurish picture in front of senior management.
- o Justify every request and number in the budget itself. Match requested increases to the company growth rate. Keep operational budget increases in line with the rate of inflation.

In Summary

Getting IT budget approval may be an uphill battle this year. Why? Simply said, times are getting tougher. The economic downturn is causing many companies to ask IT leaders to reduce their budgets. Follow the seven recommendations listed above to for better probability to secure budgetary approval.

Reduce Outsourcing Risk with Better Contract Verbiage

Research shows that over 50% of small to mid-sized enterprise (SMEs) outsourcing projects fail to meet expectations. Increase your chance of project success by using better contract verbiage to mitigate outsourcing risks.

What Are the Risks?

A successful outsourcing contract must be flexible to ensure that the evolving business needs of a typical SME can be accommodated within the contractual relationship. In an attempt to develop a flexible contract, however, many organizations forget to identify risks and fail to build risk mitigation tactics into the contract. As a result, the outsourcer and the company providing the service cannot respond effectively when a risk arises.

During the contract development phase, the organization's main objective is to negotiate a low-risk relationship that can be managed based on business-driven service levels. Building the following key sections into an outsourcing contract will increase the organization's ability to mitigate risk:

- Audit
- Innovation
- Key personnel
- Out-of-scope work
- Subcontractor approval
- Schedules and deliverables
- Term
- Termination and migration

Recommendations

Use the following list to think through the potential risks in an outsourcing relationship and arrive at contract clauses that help secure the best deal for the organization.

1. **Audit the work provided by the vendor.** Some government regulations, such as Sarbanes-Oxley legislation, state that outsourcers are obligated to provide audit information and that the service provider needs to assist with this requirement.

- Service providers must comply with Statement on Auditing Standards (SAS) No. 70, an internationally recognized auditing standard developed by the American Institute of Certified Public Accountants (AICPA). A SAS 70 audit shows that a service provider has been through an in depth audit of their control activities, which generally include controls over information technology and related processes.
- Ensure that the service has appropriate inspection windows and that it conforms to any applicable government regulations.

2. **Approve key service personnel.** Larger SMEs with significant purchasing power are granted the right to approve and disapprove of the personnel servicing their account. This enables these organizations to ensure that the vendor's service agent is customer focused. Some companies have also specified that key personnel must remain on the account for a certain number of months to ensure staff consistency.

3. **Create a process for new work beyond the scope of the contract.** Ensure that new service requirements do not, by default, go to a service provider currently under contract. In order to ensure the organization receives appropriate additional resources and market pricing for out of scope work, create a clear competitive bid procedure.

4. **Define schedules and deliverables.** Outsourced projects frequently encounter cost over runs and missed delivery schedules. Mitigate this risk by:
- Defining the project schedule and related deliverables in the contract.
- Monitoring schedules and deliverables to flag future problems.
- Inserting appropriate penalties for missed deadlines or poor service quality.

5. **Build in subcontractor approval.** For organizations that have had negative experiences with specific service

131

providers, ensure future vendors exclude these same service providers as subcontractors. Mitigate this risk by stating in the contract your right to approve any subcontractors that are used.

6. **Avoid excessively long contract terms.** The duration of an outsourcing agreement generally varies with the dollar amount, complexity, and impact of the deal. The bigger, more complex, and higher impact the outsourcing, the longer the duration. Most large outsourcing agreements for data centers, networks, or applications run five years and often seven years. For smaller outsourcings of limited and specific IT elements, such as PCs, help desk, or bulk printing, a three-year contract term is more appropriate. In general, shorter contracts favor the buyer and longer contracts favor the outsourcer. However, buyers will pay more for a specific unit of service in a short-term contract.

7. **Spend as much time considering how to exit an agreement as how to enter it.** Think through and define all cases where service levels fall below a threshold that is deemed unacceptable. If the fault cannot be remedied in a timely and effective manner it becomes cause for termination. Make sure that the vendor is contractually bound to support your migration to a new supplier or to an in-house environment.

In Summary

IT groups in SMEs are increasingly looking to outsourcing as a cost reduction vehicle. Although significant savings and efficiencies can be realized, it is important to identify and mitigate risks associated with outsourcing. This can only be done through a clear, comprehensive, and solid outsourcing contract.

ROI Produces Greater IT Success

Many IT departments in mid-sized enterprises are not using ROI calculations to justify spending decisions. Companies using ROI system enjoy a higher level of project success, and improved business alignment. You can maximize IT's value to the organization by implementing a structured ROI system.

Making the Case for ROI

In a recent survey, only 27% of over 1,500 respondents say they use ROI calculations to drive their spending decisions. This is surprising given the importance of aligning IT decisions with business objectives. Even more surprising is that over one-third have no ROI system in place and no plans to develop one. This stands in a direct contrast to Fortune 1000 companies, where performing an ROI calculation is a prerequisite for IT spending.

So why are so few mid-sized enterprises using ROI?

- Mid-sized enterprises do not have the necessary resources to implement an ROI process.
- Many managers do not have the business skills to use ROI.
- Executives do not understand and/or enforce on IT the business processes required to improve spending decisions.
- Executives feel "close to the business" and believe they intuitively know which projects have more value.

Be assured that an IT department not using some kind of ROI calculation to justify spending decisions is doing a disservice to itself and the enterprise. IT decision makers working for a mid-sized enterprise have an excellent opportunity to gain a competitive advantage over competitors by implementing an ROI process. Organizations using an ROI system enjoy the following benefits:

- Increased IT/business alignment.
- Improved investment decisions.
- Increased project success.

How to Perform an ROI Calculation

1. **The ground rules.** There are some important ground rules to keep in mind before calculating ROI.
   - ROI should be used to compare potential projects with other internal decisions and benchmarks, not with those of other companies.
   - Every ROI calculation should follow the same methodology and be a requirement for all technology reviews and investments.
2. **ROI basics.** ROI is the average of the net benefits divided by the initial cost of the project, multiplied by 100. For example, if an IT investment cost $100 and returned $200 in one year, the ROI for year one would be 200/100 x 100 = 200%. Most of the time it takes more than a year for an IT investment to recover its costs.
   - To improve ROI accuracy, I recommend using a three-year horizon. ROI over a three-year horizon is now equal to:

   ROI = (((net year 1 + net year 2 + net year 3)/3)/Initial cost) x 100

3. **Gather costs.** Although gathering costs is the easiest part of an ROI calculation, be careful to exclude costs that are not directly related to the project. Avoid confusion by following these three rules:
   - Count everything directly related to the investment.
   - Count infrastructure items that were driven by the investment.
   - Do not count infrastructure items not associated with the investment.
4. **Allocate costs.** Spread your costs across the following six cost categories, remembering that some costs are one time and others are recurring.
   - **Software,** including maintenance.
   - **Hardware,** including maintenance.

- o **Personnel.** Calculate the internal resource time required in hours and multiply by the chargeback rate.
- o **Consulting.** This is often a recurring cost.
- o **Training.** Calculate the number of hours each employee is required to spend in training. Include all the expenses involved with hiring a trainer.
- o **Other.** Allocate all outstanding costs here.
5. **Gather direct benefits.** Direct benefits are tangible savings. Some examples include decreasing paper costs, decreasing direct mail costs, selling hardware, or reducing and/or reassigning staff.
- o **Tip:** Some savings are one-time (selling old hardware), while others are recurring (decreased paper costs). Recurring savings should be included in all three years.
6. **Gather indirect benefits.** Indirect benefits are a result of increased productivity. Some examples include reducing data input time by 25%, or reducing the time required for knowledge workers to find pertinent business documents from two hours per week to fifteen minutes per week.
- o **Tip:** Be careful not to double-count an indirect benefit. If an enterprise expects to increase sales by 15% because of a new CRM system, the ROI calculation should not include both the profit on the increased sales and the value of their sales force becoming 5% more efficient. It is reasonable to assume that the sales group's increased productivity caused the increase in profit. Counting the more direct result (profit) is always better than counting the indirect result (increased productivity).

In Summary

IT departments not using ROI to justify spending decisions are doing themselves and the enterprise a disservice. Implement an ROI process to improve project success and IT/business alignment.

Return On Time Invested

You've had to call more meetings than you care to remember. How many of them actually required your staff's presence? Luckily, there is a way to increase the effectiveness of meetings your people need to attend, plus identify those meetings they don't. Learn how the Return on Time Invested (ROTI) method can do this for you.

How Does ROTI Work?

ROTI works by identifying the effectiveness or ineffectiveness of a given time commitment. The key here is that each participant ranks the meeting after it's over. A record is kept of the results and measures taken to ensure that future meetings are more productive, and held only for those whose attendance is actually required.

Why Use It?

The whole point of using the ROTI method is to maximize your workers' time. By identifying areas where a worker's time is being wasted, the more time they will have to spend on critical areas that really need attention. Saved time, arguably, means saved money and effort.

Finding the Effectiveness

It could very well be that some attendants will rank a meeting very highly, while others will find no value at all in the very same meeting. That's totally fine and no reflection on the meeting itself or the person who organized it. It's simply that the ones who rank the meeting as a poor personal ROTI probably shouldn't have been there in the first place.

An effective meeting is one where the attendants derive some benefit from being there. Benefits can include gaining valuable information, decisions reached, problems solved, or the creation of a workable schedule. Participants subjectively rank their own personal ROTI using the following scale:

0 = Without Value: No benefits received from the meeting; a total waste of time.

1 = Negative Experience: Time invested produced little benefit.

2 = Balanced, or Breakeven: Time invested equal to benefit(s) received.

3 = Positive Experience: Benefits derived that will save work or time; good ROTI.

4 = Excellent Return: Benefits gained exceed the amount of time invested.

Action Plan

Once the scores have been collected, it's time to analyze them and act upon the results. These steps will help you gauge prior meeting success as well as maximize the efficiency of future gatherings.

1. **Don't rank anything yourself.** The ROTI method is an exercise for saving staff time, not necessarily your own. Refrain from doing any ranking on your part. Instead, use the feedback you receive from participants to increase the ROTI of future meetings. Once you have tuned meetings to better suit their audiences, your efforts will not have been in vain.
2. **Tally up the scores.** You will need to find out why participants ranked the meeting the way they did. Ask specific questions directed to different levels of attendants' personal ROTI ranking, and try to elicit answers that are as detailed as possible:
   o **High Rankers (3 or 4) -** How exactly did the meeting help boost their productivity? How will they use the

information gleaned from the meeting to improve something?

- ○ **Low Rankers (0 or 1)** - At what point did they realize that the meeting was wrong for them? How could ranking be improved for the next meeting?
- ○ **Middle Rankers (2)** - What else should meetings hold for them? What other feedback can you glean from the attendants? By the way, if most people felt the meeting was a breakeven for their time spent there, consider it a mild success.
3. **Next time, publish an agenda.** You'd think that this is an obvious step, but its blatancy makes it one of the most overlooked aspects of organizing a meeting, often with disastrous consequences. If, that is, you consider wasted time a disaster. Every meeting should have a single agenda clearly spelled out ahead of time. This helps immensely in eliminating unnecessary attendance and wasting people's time.
4. **Invite only the right people.** What's the point of having a meeting whose goal is to reach a decision when the room is full of people who don't have the authority to make any changes? People like to be informed, yes, but don't cloud the issue at hand by pulling in folks who, in actuality, have nothing to do whatsoever with the situation.
5. **Decide when meetings are appropriate.** Let's say several workgroups each need to be assigned a particular task. If the tasks are disparate enough, then each group's time will be siphoned away once their specific job has been addressed, especially if they have to sit through another half hour hearing about other tasks that have nothing to do with them. Consider sending out an e-mail instead that outlines each of the tasks in detail. Better yet, schedule separate meetings for each group. Make the best use of employees' time.

In Summary
If you really want to cut costs, then try to save your staff members from pointless or unproductive meetings. Use the Return on Time Invested method and a healthy dose of common sense to achieve such a goal.

Secrets of IT Productivity

It is often taken for granted that investments in information technology will yield increases in productivity. However, providing proof that these supposed productivity boosts actually exist is often far more difficult than making the initial claims. Learn how technology investments affect productivity and determine what you need to do to extract greater productivity improvements from your IT assets.

The average information and technology user spends on average 3 hours and 15 minutes per day using technology to process work related information.

Percentages:

E-mail = 45% | IM/Text Messages = 5% | Voicemail = 19%

Conference Calls = 5% | Portal Website = 8% | Shared Networks = 18%

Providing technologies without a clear plan as to how they will improve productivity could work against you. The worry now is that, contrary to popular belief, IT investments may actually be decreasing productivity, as information workers become overwhelmed by information overload. Up to forty percent of an eight-hour workday is now spent using technology to process information. Mind you, these are not frivolous activities, such as messaging friends or shopping online - these are legitimate business activities, which include relationship management, product-lifecycle management, and e-commerce.

Information worker defined: "People who use technology and work with information in the contexts of their jobs." Information workers now represent up to 70 percent of the American workforce, or about 100 million workers in the U.S.

You Can't Manage What You Can't Measure

Measuring how employee efficiency and output is affected by technology is the first step toward figuring out how technological investments can be used to improve information worker productivity. Measuring productivity also helps managers avoid technology hype and make purchasing decisions that benefit the organization.

Action Plan

Use the following advice to help you uncover the relationship between IT and productivity in your organization.

1. **Make knowledge management a strategic objective.** A key component of personal productivity is the management of personal information and knowledge. Can you measure how employees manage their personal information? It is a very personal issue, but an issue that must be taken into consideration. In a recent survey, 41 percent of respondents indicated that they receive little or no help from their organizations in managing their personal information. Managers must change this trend by explicitly addressing productivity in corporate initiatives. They must find ways to manage information, monitor its usage, and integrate data across all user tools, including laptops, desktops, handheld devices, cell phones, and so on.
2. **Measure what you can.** While traditional methods of measuring output per hour worked are becoming increasingly obsolete in the information age, managers must try to establish some metrics that measure productivity improvements, as they relate to specific technologies. For any new technology:
   o Develop metrics that clearly trace performance (individual and process) to technology adoption. For example, how specifically will adopting a new CRM system improve the client acquisition process? Improve sales reps' call numbers?
   o Estimate how much additional time will be required by employees to use the tool and how much process redesign is required.
   o Determine the amount of additional output (this will be the most difficult to quantify) is required to make using the tool worthwhile (e.g. fewer defects, greater number

of sales, administrative tasks completed in less time, shorter meetings, reduced throughput times, accelerated project timelines). Also, outline any intangible or "soft" benefits gained from using the technology (e.g. improved social interaction, better communication, employee and customer satisfaction). Gauge how much additional complexity will be added to the system. As complexity increases, the cost of implementing new technologies increases exponentially. So, while individual technologies might only account for small portions of an information worker's time, the time spent managing the overall complexity of the system can dramatically undermine any productivity gains achieved by using individual technologies.

3. **Don't be drowning in information, but starved for knowledge.** Don't confuse information creation with productivity gains. Information does not, in and of itself, improve productivity, and can actually harm productivity as workers become overwhelmed with vast amounts of data. The role of technology should be to put this information to work (i.e. support decision-making, improve communication, act as a catalyst for product or process innovation) without adding significant amounts of additional labor overhead. The ultimate goal should be to bring the rate of increase in data in line with the rate at which the companies can actually integrate, analyze, and use this data.

4. **Evaluate IT's role in new product development.** In new development initiatives, IT investments carry the potential of boosting the design team's productivity by improving access to customer information (i.e. preferences, behaviors, feedback), thus reducing the cost and risk of developing new products. Measure IT productivity in this area by tracking requirements gathering costs, product failure rates, design reworks, speed of adoption, and overall sales.

5. **Evaluate the productivity of virtual teams.** This is one instance where IT is widely seen as contributing positively to productivity and team success. While interpersonal and logistic challenges (scheduling, varying time zones, limited synchronous communication, etc.) remain, the productivity gains in terms of

knowledge sharing and collaboration are more than apparent.

6. **Rein in e-mail abuse.** Is e-mail still the 'killer app' it once was? Many say "no." consider that the average information worker manages more than three e-mail accounts, sends 17 e-mail messages a day, receives 44, and spends about 20 percent of their total workday using e-mail applications. At the very least, users need to be filtering e-mail, using folders, limiting personal e-mail use, and identifying instances where a simple conversation may be more efficient and desirable than drawn out e-mail threads.

7. **Get beyond the technology to usage and behavior.** Technology is only one half of the story. The other key factor in the productivity percentage is people. To take full advantage of the technology that you already have, you must train information workers on information management tools and techniques, coach them on how to perform key tasks effectively, and motivate them to give it their all while on the job.

In Summary

Competitive advantage comes not from IT investment, but rather from the way in which IT enables information work. Make sure that you can measure this relationship in order to manage it.

SLA's Improve Alignment

In the absence of an internal Service Level Agreement (SLA), business users often expect unlimited IT support at any time, with no conditions. Unrestricted service demands set IT up for failure in the eyes of users and business executives. Set clear simple service levels to align user demand with the IT group's ability to deliver.

The Benefits of an Internal SLA

An internal SLA is an agreement that spells out the terms of service that the IT department will provide to the enterprise. Contrary to popular belief an SLA does not restrict demand for IT services - rather it attempts to define the demand and match IT resources to meet it.

Organizations in favor of structuring the delivery of IT services around an SLA argue that the document improves IT alignment by doing the following:

- Setting clear and deliverable service expectations.
- Transforming a technology-focused staff into customer-friendly business partners.
- Building trust between business users and IT staff.
- Increasing user satisfaction with IT.
- Establishing baselines for performance against which IT staff can be evaluated.
- Explaining to the business exactly what IT does with its resource allocation, and defines the value it gets from those resources.

The Cons

IT decision makers who oppose the internal SLA believe that the agreement perpetuates the notion that IT employees are service providers rather than business partners. Although this appears to be a valid concern, IT must remember that every department provides a service to the business. And in most situations a business department is expected to deliver agreed-upon service objectives.

Credible managers use metrics to provide executives with visibility into a department's level of performance. SLAs provide IT managers with the metrics required to quantify the value IT is delivering to the enterprise.

SLA Case Scenario

An IT manager working for an SME with a annual IT budget of $500,000, used a help desk SLA to prevent business leaders from cutting the help desk by 20% during a budget review. The SLA provided the IT manager with the visibility into IT performance, service, and support costs.

The transparency of this information allowed IT to objectively explain the impact that a 20% cut would have on the expected level of service the help desk provides. As a result, the help desk was only cut by 5%.

Recommendations

1. **Obtain buy-in from business leaders.** Executives must understand that the purpose of an internal SLA is not to restrict user demand, but rather to define demand and align IT resources to meet these demands. Applying supply and demand economics to IT service delivery allows IT to translate user demand into the cost required to meet that demand.
2. **Obtain IT department buy-in.** Selling IT staff on the value of internal SLAs at the onset is critical. Be prepared to drive a culture change with an emphasis on service.
    *   Outline the value of IT transparency and how it will increase the department's profile within the enterprise.
    *   Explain how the baselines established in the SLA will let them know exactly where they stand in terms of their performance.
3. **Get IT support staff to draft the SLA.** Increase buy-in by assigning some control of the SLA to the people who

will be held accountable for meeting the SLA. Prevent individuals from setting service levels too low by establishing the following conditions:

- Business users must sign off on the SLA.
- Managers will review the SLA to ensure it adequately stretches IT's abilities.

4. **Start with the help desk.** In order to figure out what service levels the IT support staff should make, start with the lifecycle of a help desk ticket, the kinds of calls fielded by the help desk, and the average response times.

- Identify the total number of tickets that are generated on any given day.
- Categorize help desk calls by request type (such as a hardware or software issue).
- Assign a level of urgency (that is, whether the call was a high, medium, or low priority).

5. **Focus on business objectives.** Weigh priorities against business goals. For example, in a manufacturing company, any call having to do with the Supply Chain Management (SCM) system will qualify as a high priority since an optimal supply chain is a core part of manufacturing.

6. **Use appropriate wording.** In order to ensure an SLA advocates a business partnership, it is essential that all of the services described in the SLA are oriented toward the business user. It is easy to write the document as a contract rather than what it really is, an agreement. Although it may be easy or even desirable for IT to stipulate the terms of a service and outline specific exclusions, if end users have trouble reading it, they will have difficulty following or understanding the terms.

In Summary

Manage end-user expectations and provide transparency into the value IT provides the business. Use an internal SLA to set service levels and align IT with business objectives.

Strategic Procurement

Strategic Procurement Part One:

A focus on strategic procurement is helping CIOs of large organizations improve bottom-line performance. Take the first step towards making procurement a competitive advantage for your IT department by assessing the strategic maturity of your procurement practices.

A Dynamic Field

Procurement's increasing importance is being driven by two economic changes:

- Increasing competitive pressures are forcing companies to look at procurement as a means of helping boost the bottom line. CEOs are looking for areas to cut costs, and streamlining procurement processes is a viable solution.
- A lot of companies are doing more outsourcing. This makes procurement decisions increasingly important to business vitality.

There are numerous ways an effective procurement strategy improves performance, including:

- Eliminating maverick spending.
- Streamlining operations.
- Improving supplier relationships.
- Increasing bargaining power with suppliers.
- Strengthening supplier relationships.
- Aligning purchasing decisions with corporate goals and objectives.

How Mature Are You?

Measuring an organization's procurement maturity involves assessing how close it is to achieving each of the aforementioned results. There are four levels of maturity:

novice, intermediate, advanced, and expert. There is no relationship between company size and procurement maturity. Companies of all sizes are at various stages in the development of their procurement functions.

Maturity Assessment Guide

1. **Evaluate maverick spending in the IT department.** Talk to supervisors and find out if unauthorized purchases are being made. If so, what kind of purchases? You may be shocked by the number of purchases occurring outside of formal procurement protocols. On the other hand, with no protocol in place, expect excessive amounts of maverick spending. Procurement maturity is typically characterized by the following levels of maverick spending:
   o Level 1: Significant maverick spending.
   o Level 2: Minimal maverick spending.
   o Level 3: Virtually no maverick spending.
   o Level 4: No maverick spending.
2. **Examine your procurement processes and procedures.** Find your written set of procedures detailing the procurement processes for your company. If there is no documentation, does your company follow repeatable procedures? Or does each purchase result in an ad-hoc patchwork of steps? Procurement maturity is typically characterized by the following levels of procurement procedures:
   o Level 1: No processes or procedures.
   o Level 2: Processes and procedures exist, but are not documented.
   o Level 3: Processes and procedures are documented and implemented.
   o Level 4: Major procurement decisions are determined by a multi-function team.
3. **Evaluate your relationship with suppliers.** Look beyond your internal procurement processes and focus on how well you know your suppliers. Typically, the more information you have about the people you do business with, the better the relationship. With no purchase information on hand, you cannot develop a partnership with suppliers and service providers. With proper

147

information, you can evaluate and rank suppliers. Your procurement maturity level relates to your supplier relationships as follows:

- Level 1: No purchase information on record; need to ask suppliers for it.
- Level 2: Use supplier information to evaluate price, quality, and delivery.
- Level 3: Rank suppliers and develop strong relationships with select suppliers.
- Level 4: A supplier's percentage of business correlates with performance ranking.

4. **Assess your bargaining power.** Information also provides you with purchasing leverage. To what degree do you leverage information about suppliers to increase spending power? Do you coordinate purchases to increase leverage? Does your company possess strong negotiating skills? Your procurement maturity level is characterized by your ability to leverage spending power:

- Level 1: Company spending power is not leveraged.
- Level 2: Major purchases are negotiated and coordinated to increase leverage.
- Level 3: All purchases are coordinated and leveraged.
- Level 4: Supplier's cost-reduction ideas are brought to your company first.

5. **Determine procurement's strategic alignment.** Experienced buyers understand the overall corporate strategy and the procurement strategy. How many of your buying decisions are viewed as strategic decisions? Do you have a strategic plan in place? Procurement's strategic alignment relates to maturity as follows:

- Level 1: No strategic plan governing procurement.
- Level 2: Although no strategic plan exists, purchases are strategically relevant.
- Level 3: Virtually all purchases are aligned with corporate strategy.
- Level 4: Perfect alignment with company goals and objectives.

6. **Evaluate your buying experience.** Do your buyers receive training? Do they understand the strategic relevance of buying decisions? Do they know how to apply cost accounting to a negotiation? For example, do

they know the difference between direct and indirect costs, as well as overhead? Your procurement maturity level with respect to buying experience is characterized as follows:

o   Level 1: Limited buying experience; no training.
o   Level 2: Buyer training program is in place.
o   Level 3 & 4: Buyers understand strategic buying and the importance of cost.

In Summary

A strategic approach to IT procurement can help cut costs and improve efficiencies. The first step to taking a strategic approach to IT procurement strategy is assessing your current procurement maturity.

Strategic Procurement Part Two:

Many enterprises have gained a strategic advantage by treating their procurement as a strategic function. Map out your procurement process and make sure it encompasses these best practices.

Strong procurement processes align purchasing decisions with corporate strategy, increase bargaining power with suppliers, and increase the value obtained from investments.

The key is determining when to put procurement through a detailed process. The dollar value of the purchase is always a strong indicator of strategic relevance. For example, ordering all of office supplies from one supplier at predetermined intervals can increase purchasing leverage. More obvious examples include replacing 50 CRT monitors with LCD monitors, purchasing 30 handheld devices, investing in a storage area network, or establishing a wireless local area network. To achieve maximum value from purchases such as these, a procurement protocol must be followed.

Best Practices

Add the following best practices to your current procurement procedures to minimize maverick spending, maximize operational efficiency, achieve substantial bargaining power with suppliers, and align purchasing decisions with corporate goals and objectives.

1. **Establish the procurement goal.**
   o Define the target consumer and the borders of the area impacted by the purchase as precisely as possible (i.e. dependencies on other projects, items and systems, the effects on business processes, etc.).
   o Determine whether the purchase is aligned with corporate goals and objectives. If the argument for the purchase cannot be justified along strategic lines, save yourself a lot of work by aborting the purchase and turning your focus toward more strategically relevant procurements.
   o Interview stakeholders and analyze their stakes in the procurement.
   o Analyze costs and benefits.
2. **Define procurement requirements.** The most important part of the procurement process is planning out the details of the purchase. Keeping in mind that even good plans are susceptible to change, it is essential to ensure thorough version management of the goal and plan during the whole process. The list of requirements demands completion of the following activities:
   o Determine scenarios for receiving the product or service from the supplier.
   o Analyze the risks involved in the purchase.
   o Plan the procurement within a risk management framework.
   o Identify the main decision points, including timelines, type of supplier, type of tendering, flexibility of contracts, and project requirements.
3. **Tender the offer.** The objective of tendering is to select a supplier, and agree with a chosen supplier on a contract that defines deliverables and the

responsibilities of both parties. The following activities are required to complete this step:

o Evaluating the previous performance of suppliers (if the information is available).
o Preparing a request for proposal (RFP).
o Evaluating the suppliers' response proposals.
o Selecting the supplier that best meets the strategic needs of the organization.
o Preparing a supplier contract for the delivery of products or services.

4. **Monitor supplier deliverables.** This step aims to monitor the procurement objective as defined in the contract, i.e. to ensure that the deliverables conform to the requirements. Therefore, a defined number of contract status reports should be prepared during the project. The purpose of these reports is to minimize the risk of unfulfilled contract obligations, and to build a performance knowledge base of the supplier.

5. **Complete the procurement.** This task ensures that all outstanding issues regarding the procurement have been concluded to your satisfaction. Activities to perform include:

o Ensure all contracts are completed.
o Assess the achievement of the procurement goal.
o Evaluate the results for future procurements, including supplier quality and areas to improve the procurement process.

In Summary

A strong procurement strategy aligns purchasing decisions with corporate strategy, increases bargaining power with suppliers, and boosts the value obtained from investments. In order to develop your procurement function, focus on processes and people.

Strong Business Alignment for IT

The better aligned your IT organization is with the enterprise's business plans, the more valuable IT's contribution to the bottom line will be. Improve IT/business alignment by mapping IT project decisions to the enterprise's goals and objectives.

The Importance of IT/Business Alignment

A recent survey used the following questions to gauge the degree of IT/business alignment in the mid-sized enterprise:

- Are the business and IT aligned?
- Do you have enough time with senior management?
- Does IT drive competitive advantage?
- Does business management understand IT?

Results reveal that in most companies a large gap exists between the business and IT groups. When asked if they agreed, disagreed, or felt neutral about how each of the preceding questions applied to their current situation, a majority of respondents felt neutral. For an IT decision maker to consider him or herself a successful IT professional, they must be in full agreement with each of these questions. Neutrality is not an option.

The Impact of Effective Planning

The purpose of business planning is to create consensus across the enterprise on strategic direction and a framework for making key decisions. IT can maximize its contribution to bottom line performance by aligning its function with the goals and objectives of the business plan.

The best way to improve alignment is by mapping IT project decisions to whatever level of planning the enterprise is capable of. This could be a two to three year strategic plan, a ten to twelve month tactical plan, or simply a prioritized list of upcoming projects.

The benefits of IT/business alignment are straightforward, but worth listing.

Aligned	Not Aligned
Access to business executives.	Lack of access to key business decision makers.
IT plays an important role in the enterprise's strategic planning process.	IT has a limited role in the enterprise's strategic planning process.
Investment decisions are proactive and maximize IT's opportunity to create a competitive advantage.	Investment decisions are reactive leading to minimal opportunities to build IT into a competitive advantage.
High level of project success.	Low level of project success.

Recommendations

1. **Obtain key stakeholder buy-in and locate governing business plan.** Due to the impact of aligning IT investment decisions with business priorities, C-level involvement is vital. Without upfront buy-in from the senior management team, your alignment efforts will be thwarted before they begin. Talk to senior managers about the business plan guiding their efforts and ask to see supporting documentation.
o A business plan could be as advanced as a three year strategic plan, or as simple as a project list.
2. **Be prepared to make the case for IT/business alignment.** You may need to justify spending the time and resources required to align IT investment decisions with the enterprise's goals and objectives. Use the following points to bolster your case.
o **Better project tracking and budgeting.** Organizations aligned with the business plan are more

likely to finish their projects on time and on budget than those organizations not utilizing this practice.

o **Increased project success.** Organizations aligned with the business plan improve their chances of project success by over 60 percent.

o **Increased ability to obtain funding.** Over 75 percent of organizations that align their investment decisions with the business plan increase their ability to obtain funding for new IT initiatives.

o **Increased competitiveness.** Seventy-five percent of organizations that make IT/business alignment a priority are more competitive than organizations that do not.

3. **Align investment decisions with the business plan.** This helps IT decision makers develop and publish a strategic and tactical IT plans that are aligned with the goals and objectives of the enterprise.

4. **Obtain sign off from key stakeholders.** After aligning IT's investment decisions with the business plan, the results need to be communicated to business executives. Be prepared to clarify and justify how each investment decision aligns with the business plan.

In Summary

Aligning IT with the business should be a top management priority for IT decision makers. Find out what plans are guiding business executives, and map all IT investment decisions to them.

Tactical vs. Strategic

Knowing when a project has strategic implications makes the difference between meeting business expectations and project failure. This inability to differentiate is a key contributor to the rampant misalignment of IT and business in small- to mid-sized enterprises (SMEs). Improve IT's success ratio by understanding from the outset whether a project is tactical or strategic in nature.

Strategic Awareness Is a Manager's Responsibility

Every business has a strategy, even if it is not formally documented. The projects that a business engages in offer a clear reflection of strategic intent.

Most SME businesses lack the time and resources required to capture and document a majority of the management decisions being made. The management team is too busy to get involved in most departmental project decisions. This puts the onus on executives and managers in every area of the company.

Successful companies are run by a management team that understands project decisions required to keep the company moving in the right direction. Unfortunately, most IT decision makers are so caught up in day-to-day operations they cannot distinguish the difference between tactical and strategic projects.

Strategic vs. Tactical

Although few SME businesses can hand their IT managers a three-to five-year strategic plan, most will have a list of prioritized projects. The IT decision maker needs to obtain this information and understand the business drivers for each. This awareness helps IT add business value by:

- Identifying technology solutions that satisfy multiple business objectives.

155

- Minimizing future costs by addressing additional functionality and scalability.
- Leveraging a project to introduce new ways of automating processes.

Once the CIO has a list of projects and understands the business driver of each, he or she will have a good idea which are strategic and which are tactical. In general, strategic projects are long-term and drive the business forward, while tactical projects are short-term and maintain or improve current operations. The table below provides a rough blueprint for project profiling.

Project Type	Strategic	Tactical
Project Goal	-Competitive advantage -Decreased costs -Increased revenue/profit -Launch new product/service	-Business continuity -Satisfy regulation -Security -Strategic components -System upgrades
Time Frame	3 to 24 months	1 to 6 months
Complexity	High	Low to medium

Case Study: Expanding ERP Functionality

A prominent manufacturer recently deployed a large Enterprise Resource Planning (ERP) upgrade. The upgrade included the addition of accounts receivable and accounts payable modules, multi-currency handling, and integration with a Web-based, client-facing e-commerce solution.

The project started when the CEO gave the green light to the finance department's request for an accounts receivable module. Instead of immediately putting his nose to the grindstone and finding the best solution for the organization's existing ERP system, the IT manager asked senior management about the project driver. Senior management revealed its plans to double revenue in the next two years. It would do so by expanding its product line and moving into foreign markets. It also wanted to provide clients with the opportunity to purchase items through the Web site.

The strategic implications of the finance department's project request were clear – automated invoicing would allow the enterprise to increase the number of transactions it could process without increasing head count. The IT manager realized that this ERP project was much more complex than adding an accounts receivable module. He posed some serious questions to senior management:

- What if the current ERP system cannot handle the transactions required to double revenue?
- Should the company use this opportunity to automate accounts payable?
- Will the move into foreign markets require multi-currency handling?

  This was a strategic project, and the IT manager had the ear of senior management. He recognized three important ways IT could add substantial value to the business:

- Upgrading the overall ERP system would satisfy multiple business objectives.
- Adding an accounts payable module and multi-currency handling would give the organization leverage with the vendor and save costs.
- Integrating the ERP system with the Website.

The senior management team was pleased with these synergies and the IT manager had little difficulty obtaining executive buy-in. Once IT received commitment, he broke the project into a series of smaller, manageable components. The strategic project became a series of tactical projects. In addition to addressing compliance, security, and disaster recovery, tactical projects provide the subset of milestones required to complete a strategic project.

While ERP expansion was a long-term strategic project, IT would employ the following tactics to complete the project.

- Complete a feasibility study of the current infrastructure to decide whether to upgrade the current system or buy a new system.
- Develop a project plan.
- Complete a Request for Proposal (RFP) and send it to the appropriate vendors.
- Implement the upgrade or the new ERP system.

In Summary

Knowing the difference between a tactical project and a strategic project increases IT's value to the business.

To Get a Good Vendor Be a Better Customer

It's not uncommon to be frustrated with a vendor. But what are CIOs doing to improve the situation? By treating vendors like strategic partners, CIOs are in a better position to get what they need from the relationship.

It's Up to the Customer

CIOs who want to receive better service from a vendor must treat the relationship like a strategic partnership. And, contrary to common opinion, the onus is actually on the customer to make this happen. The customer is the one who begins the relationship, and the one who decides when and how it will end. CIOs who are good customers forge win-win relationships with their vendors, and are able to facilitate meaningful business discussions and quick problem resolutions.

On the flip side, vendors that can meet their own strategic goals through a relationship with a customer are motivated to ensure that the customer remains satisfied. For example, a customer may be able to negotiate a lower price for products or services if they participate in a customer case study success story.

How to Be a Good Customer

Use these guidelines to improve the vendor-customer relationship, and get the most from the alliance.

1. **Find common ground.** Vendors and buyers must be in sync in terms of the perceived economic impact of the product or service being procured. A purchase that is a huge investment for the enterprise and of critical importance for business success must be of similar value to the vendor. If the vendor sees the purchase as a small account, then the relationship will never play out to anyone's satisfaction.

2. **Check references.** Before beginning a relationship with a vendor, check their references:
   o Watch out for Jekyll and Hyde vendors that say they're committed to a partnership during the sale, but ignore their customers after purchase. Ask customer references specifically about the vendor's pre- and post-purchase attitude towards establishing partnerships with their customers.
   o If customer references indicate that the vendor doesn't take the time to establish a solid relationship, then trying to establish a partnership will be futile. Abandon a partnership approach or move on to another vendor.
3. **Establish credibility.** CIOs should have their operational managers talk to vendors before establishing a relationship. If a vendor is selling a development tool, then they should present it to the application development manager. If it is a network appliance, then they should be talking to the network manager. Once credibility has been established with operational managers, the vendors can meet with the CIO.
   o Many enterprises host an annual all-day meeting with their top vendors to discuss the enterprise's short- and long-term business goals. They brainstorm ways to help the enterprise be successful as a group.
   o CIOs must be up front with vendors on pet peeves. For instance, many CIOs stress the importance of one point of contact with each vendor. This helps formalize vendor accountability.
4. **Tell the vendor how to be successful.** Share with the vendor the enterprise's IT and business goals. Educate them on how to work successfully with the company.
5. **Understand the goals of the vendor.** While a vendor needs to understand the goals of its customers, CIOs must understand what motivates their vendors. The vendor's success ensures the customer's success. Profitable customer accounts can expect to receive higher levels of service. For instance:
   o The vendor representative communicates to the customer that he is eligible for extra OEM incentives if the customer commits to a product purchase by a certain date. In turn, the customer shares with the vendor that the business group will not commit without a 24/7

hardware support contract. The customer can accommodate the procurement date if the vendor will commit to the improved support terms. By communicating goals, both the vendor and customer are able to get what they need from the relationship. This creates goodwill, ensuring a productive future partnership.

6. **Introduce healthy competition.** CIOs need to let a vendor know that options are being kept open. Vendors must understand that best practice standards and competitive pricing are expected. Introducing competition sends the message that stagnation in products or services will not be tolerated.

7. **Use relationship management best practices.** Standardizing on a few vendors, creating a vendor management office (VMO), and utilizing relationship management software can greatly improve a CIO's chances of creating successful vendor relationships.

In Summary

Establishing a partnership that allows for the success of both the customer and the vendor results in better problem resolution and increased satisfaction. Take control of the vendor-customer relationship to increase the success of the enterprise.

Unexpected Benefits of Asset Management

Enterprises spend a large part of their budget on hardware and software and expect these assets to provide continuing value over several years. IT managers must have a clear picture of what assets the enterprise has and where they are. The broadly adopted IT Infrastructure Library (ITIL) framework for service management recognizes the importance of managing assets, within the broader category of Configuration Management.

The IT Asset Management Challenge

Because some assets can be moved (laptops and printers, for example), they can be managed only if their location is known. IT can keep equipment and software up-to-date with upgrades and patches only if it has a complete record of what it has deployed. Similarly, IT can diagnose problems quickly only if IT knows what hardware and software is in place.

IT departments should manage hardware and software assets through the stages of requisition, procurement, deployment, operation, and retirement. A typical example of poor asset management is the failure to redeploy a PC or a number of software licenses after an employee leaves.

Good asset management involves more than the tracking of assets. Before buying new equipment, consider whether the required hardware or software is already available but not used. During deployment, ensure that installation is of the right equipment with the right software to avoid rework. Use asset records to diagnose problems more quickly when there is an incident.

What an Asset Management System Can Do

Enterprises have found significant cost reductions of up to 20% by applying asset management disciplines, even with simple tools, to the following activities:

- **End-user support.** Accurate information about the hardware configuration and software versions deployed on a user device allows the help desk staff to more quickly diagnoses and repair incidents because they can skip the preliminary data gathering. Fewer staff members are required to achieve target service levels, and problems are resolved more quickly and correctly. This also enhances repeatability of a given resolution.
- **Procurement.** Information about actual devices, applications, and operating systems deployed supports cost-effective decisions on appropriate software licensing, eliminates unnecessary hardware and software purchases, and allows bulk purchasing at reduced prices.

An asset management process (and tools) that integrate with a service management process (and tools) creates additional benefits:

- **Database management.** The ability to easily identify and locate sources of data reduces the amount of labor required to find data and reduces the number of unnecessary databases and their associated support costs.
- **Operations.** Detailed knowledge of what is where leads to speedy and efficient deployment of software changes, such as patches, and faster resolution of incidents.
- **Network management.** Detailed information about how end-user devices, servers, storage, and external partners are interconnected leads to accelerated and complete deployment of changes and upgrades, and supports rapid restoration of service.

Implement Asset Management as Part of the Service Management Process

While asset management can be approached area by area (software, network, data, etc.), GSC recommends approaching it as a key part of a unified service management process. Precise information about assets reduces the cost and improves the quality of a number of different activities within IT: in particular, procurement, user support, financial management, and service restoration. An asset inventory, however, is of little use on its own. It will be effective to the extent that there is an automated linkage to the systems that support these activities.

Recommendations

1. **Acquire an asset management system that is appropriate for the enterprise's IT complexity.** Some organizations only need to track licenses. Others need to improve the costs and performance of IT equipment procurement, user support, database management, operations, and network management.
2. **Acquire an asset management system only after a service management system is in place.** If the objective for an asset management system is to improve service management, pick and install the service management piece first.
3. **Choose a system that is able to handle all types of IT assets.** The system should be capable of handling all types of IT assets, workstations, servers, network elements, and software. The process of deployment will likely be gradual, but a single universal asset inventory will simplify integration with service management.
4. **Choose a system that works well with existing procurement and service management processes.** Stay with the existing vendor if satisfactory service management tools are in place. The value of asset management lies with its impact on improved procurement and operations, more so than merely as a tool for planning.
5. **Organize the initial population of the inventory to ensure data quality.** Installing the asset management system is straightforward. The discovery of devices on the enterprise network is aided by tools available as part of the asset management system. Carry out the process in a disciplined and complete manner. An asset management system is only as good as the accuracy of its data.

In Summary

Enterprises of all sizes search for ways to reduce the cost and increase the utilization of their software and hardware assets. Employ IT asset management processes and tools not only to reduce asset costs but also to reduce the costs of service management and improve service levels.

Using Correct Metrics for the IT Scorecard

While IT must collect hundreds of metrics for internal infrastructure management, learning how to restate these in business terms remains a challenge. Tying performance scorecards to business objectives helps refocus the language to generate an emotional response from business leaders, cuts down on the length of IT performance reports, and greatly improves the reporting process.

No Metrics? Get Metrics

Enterprises not currently using metrics to manage performance have much to gain. There are many benefits to be had from an effective IT metrics program, including more sophisticated data center management, better alignment with the needs of the business, and improved competitiveness. Enterprises that use performance metrics achieve much higher levels of competitive advantage (see Figure 1). In addition, using metrics in the context of an IT performance scorecard can help IT leaders:

- Translate IT investments into informed business decisions.
- Defend funding for IT initiatives and budget increases.
- Communicate the business value of IT to senior executives.
- Improve corporate governance or compliance initiatives (e.g. ITIL, COBIT, Sarbanes-Oxley).

Wrong Metrics? Re-focus Metrics

While an effective metrics reporting program will boost performance and establish a framework for continuous improvement, ill-conceived metrics focus attention on the wrong areas and can reflect poorly on IT performance. As an example, consider how uptime metrics are often misused:

- A target of 99% uptime means little if the 1% of downtime occurs right at the time that a critical project is due.
- If a particular application is not critical and business users are content with 95% uptime, then time spent trying to achieve 99% uptime for that application means that IT is focusing its attention on the wrong area.

When developing internal reporting objectives, focus on metrics that demonstrate how IT is increasing business value to the enterprise or reducing IT cost. In general, the business wants to drive revenue growth, profit, market share, and shareholder value. The more IT can link its performance scorecard to these high level objectives, the better.

IT Scorecard	Business Objective
-Internal operational efficiency and resource optimization.	-Lower IT costs leading to greater profits.
-Improved reliability of IT infrastructure and service delivery.	-Greater user satisfaction, productivity, and retention, means lower costs and better value to customers.
-Risk reduction and mitigation through IT governance initiatives.	-Better value for shareholders.
-Greater customer satisfaction from external facing systems.	-Customer retention, revenue growth, and profitability.
-Financial accountability and positive return on investment for IT investments.	-Profitability and lower exposure to risk ultimately leading to shareholder value.

For most IT leaders, what this means is changing the way they think about metrics. Instead of using operational, technology-focused metrics for reporting purposes, they must now adopt process-focused metrics that relate to service delivery and business impact. The "right" metrics are those that evoke an emotional response from management. Consider the following examples:

Traditional Metrics: The transaction server had 98% uptime this month. IT updated software asset management software on all 500 enterprise PCs. 30% of PCs were replaced this year. 75% of help desk requests were resolved in less than 20 minutes. IT resolved 1,200 tickets this month.

Emotional Metrics: "Computer failures" affected 75 transactions this month, costing the enterprise $15,000. To fix this problem, we must invest in more server redundancy. New computer software reduced the enterprise's exposure to a license compliance risk worth $250,000 (if audited and found lacking). Computer replacements helped improve user productivity and lowered maintenance costs by $60,000 this year. Faster help desk response times resulted in 10% less downtime this quarter, saving the enterprise $20,000. 20% of IT staff time was devoted to resolving tickets. 40% of requests were related to the operating system. Windows Vista training for users could reduce the number of requests and save $5,000 per month in IT productivity.

When developing IT metrics, consider the following types used by leading enterprises:

- Business impact, including business process performance.
- Top-ten analysis by rate of occurrence, time spent, or elapsed time.
- Performance relative to Service Level Agreements (SLAs).
- Staff workload (hours worked) versus performance (output achieved).
- Trend analysis.

Too Many Metrics? Reduce Metrics

IT management tools can churn out hundreds of metrics that are necessary to help proactively prevent failures and diagnose problems. However, most of these are useless to executives unless they relate to business objectives. Analyzing and reporting on too many metrics is not only time consuming and wasteful, but it can also be dangerous. Presenting management with a laundry list of all IT metrics available can lead to information overload and cause decision makers to lose sight of those indices that are truly important for improving performance.

Quarterly IT reports that span dozens of pages and report on abstract technology-focused metrics such as volume of mainframe batch runs, megabytes of data stored, jobs processed, or number of patches installed will be meaningless to business leaders. If this is the current state, metric triage is essential.

Focus on those aspects of IT operations that draw emotional responses from business leaders, users, and customers. Think about what minimum amount of information must be conveyed to convince management that what IT is doing is right or wrong.

Recommendations

1. **Develop a service delivery strategy.** Gathering metrics is one aspect of managing IT service delivery. A properly executed service delivery model will align IT initiatives with business objectives and eliminate gaps between what IT delivers and what the business expects.
2. **Reduce the number of IT metrics reported to no more than a dozen.** Metrics are common in the IT game; distilling them down to a consumable form is the magic. To isolate those applications, processes, and systems that are important to the business, start by addressing the loudest and most often heard complaints about IT. Next, identify key areas in SLAs used by management to track IT performance. Finally, look at those IT projects that had a high impact on business processes. If metrics are not already available for any of these areas, generate a list of projects needed in order to obtain the missing data. For the majority of enterprises, quarterly IT performance reports should be no longer than a few pages and contain no more than a dozen or so high level metrics. High-level dashboards should be easy to understand. One best practice is to use "red/yellow/green" reporting. In general, management

really only cares about what is red or yellow. For these items, provide more granular metrics that identify root causes. Report on items that are green as well, but only at a high level. If it's green, no one will really care; it's business as usual.

3. **Investigate chargeback functionality in management software**. Software for managing servers and storage (for example, Symantec's Server and Storage Foundation) have options for calculating usage for chargeback. Even if there is no intention to formally chargeback for IT services, these tools can provide insight into IT service costs for conducting business analysis such as Return on Investment. For example, it may be salient for the business to know that the Storage Area Network (SAN) is a $60,000 resource or that the finance system is using 48% of the overall resource and 80% of the high-speed drives in the resource. Numbers like this can help articulate real dollar costs against which savings such as reduced downtime, deferred hardware purchases, and faster transaction processing can be measured.

4. **Identify how IT can contribute to the enterprise's competitive strategy.** Map IT activities to business processes. There are two types of activities that should be given priority:

o **Mission-critical activities.** Those activities that can result in severe negative impact to the business if compromised (e.g. securing confidential client information).

o **Competitive activities.** Those initiatives that fulfill business objectives and further the enterprise's competitive strategy.

5. **Sell IT successes.** Use emotional metrics and an internal PR process for promoting IT successes.

In Summary

Most IT departments don't use metrics, report on the wrong metrics, or gather so many metrics that presenting them in a usable manner becomes impossible. Develop a pragmatic approach to IT metrics and performance reporting.

26 Ways to Cut IT Cost

1. Focus initially on cutting "people costs": Freeze headcount, reduce/eliminate special bonuses, reduce regional support.

    37% of an average budget is spent on people costs, including money paid to contractors. Companies were planning to spend $13,454 per employee, and that is already down $200, or 1.7% per person. Painful to talk about, this area is a big target -- but use a scalpel. Keep people who ensure the greatest transmission of business knowledge.

2. Flatten organization structure: Move to collaborative, team-based models.

    More people are working in virtual teams, and the model is reducing overhead administrative costs, It's not unusual for managers who oversaw seven people to now manage between 15 and 20 people.

3. Accelerate the progress of centralized and shared services: Leverage enterprise-wide competencies, reduce staff embedded in business units.

    Organizations are seeing a 15% to 20% reduction in costs by moving to shared services. But proceed with caution. Start by benchmarking your current costs and mapping your operations, so you know who you have to keep and which people can go.

4. Bring a qualified finance person into your IT leadership team, perhaps on loan or on temporary contract.

    CIOs take a knife to their budgets, only to find the cost savings have been shifted to other business units. "Make sure these cost are really taken out," Kitzis said, by using an accounting expert. Also, tap legal expertise to review contracts for penalty clauses and other terms as you make cuts.

5. Maintain or strengthen relationship management roles: Business analysts, business process and industry experts, account executives, relationship managers.

6. Take control of "unmanaged" costs you can measure and cut easily, such as data center power consumption or printing.

    Be smart on the managed costs. Re-educate the business on service level agreements (SLAs) and let them know what happens when SLAs are reduced by 5% or 10% before making a move.

Cut costs in enterprise software (Caution ahead!)
7. Use invoice verification.

    The industry has seen a slew of acquisitions. Big vendors have snapped up small fries with 1,000 customers apiece. It's easier for them to apply their boilerplate policies to inherited customers and wait for the complaints than it is to review contracts individually. You can save 5% to 10% by correcting those invoices or play hardball when you agree to a new contract.

8. Eliminate unused software/modules.

    Understand who's using what and why. Lots of closet cleaning here.

9. Apply more sophisticated negotiations.

    "You can't put someone who bought pencils into a negotiation" with a big software vendor, "They'll get eaten alive."

10. Use alternative products included in previous deals.

    When budgets are bountiful, IT demands tools it may not need. You may have to decide between using a tool and keeping "Joe," Snyder said. Maybe in these times, you'll decide you can do without the tool.

11. Introduce competition for existing products.

You must foster vendor competition if you hope to lower costs. If you decide to switch, make sure you calculate the cost of taking out the incumbent beforehand.

12. Use "best-for-need" rather than "best-of-breed" products.

You could be paying as much as a 50% premium for best of breed.

Cut costs in enterprise infrastructure and operations: Networks and telecom

13. Use telecom expense management services (save 10% to 35%).

Nobody can keep track of this stuff. Hire a professional to source, benchmark, negotiate the contracts, etc., and audit the bills.

14. Move to corporate liability for wireless services (save 15% to 30%).

Who's responsible for the bills of individuals, what devices they use? The enterprise should take control and set standards.

15. Reduce the reliability target for a location by "one 9" (save 30%).

16. Collapse rich media conferencing into a premises-based multi-control point unit (save 60%).

As hardware costs come down, building your own videoconferencing center can save big money over the long run, assuming you do a lot of it.

17. Deploy IP telephony and Voice over Internet Protocol (save 50% to 80% of maintenance).

18. Use the Internet as corporate transport (save 10% to 80%).

Cut costs in enterprise infrastructure, hardware and IT operations
19. Defer the latest Windows PC replacements if possible.

    Three-year-old PCs and 2-year-old laptops might be able to go another year, but you should be mindful of the maintenance costs.

20. Exploit commoditization: the best-for-need instead of best-of-breed argument, redux.

21. Make better use of existing tools by improving process and policy.

    "It's not always the tool's fault.

22. Defer client architecture pilot/evaluation projects.

23. Implement thin provisioning and data de-duplication for storage reduction.

24. Consolidate and virtualize servers.

25. Implement Cloud Computing When Possible

Emerging trends in IT cost pressure
26. Target two or three areas for "zero-based budgeting."

Implement ITIL

It has become increasingly recognized that information is the most important strategic resource that any organization has to manage. Key to the collection, analysis, production and distribution of information within an organization is the quality of the IT Services provided to the business. It is essential that we
recognize that IT Services are crucial, strategic, organizational assets and therefore organizations must invest appropriate levels of resource into the support, delivery and management of these critical IT Services and the IT systems that underpin them. However, these aspects of IT are often overlooked or only superficially addressed within many organizations.

Key issues facing many of today's senior Business Managers and IT Managers are:
- IT and business strategic planning
- Integrating and aligning IT and business goals
- Implementing continual improvement
- Measuring IT organization effectiveness and efficiency
- Optimizing costs and the Total Cost of Ownership (TCO)
- Achieving and demonstrating Return on Investment (ROI)
- Demonstrating the business value of IT
- Developing business and IT partnerships and relationships
- Improving project delivery success
- Outsourcing, in sourcing and smart sourcing
- Using IT to gain competitive advantage
- Delivering the required, business justified IT services (i.e. what is required, when required and at an agreed cost)
- Managing constant business and IT change
- Demonstrating appropriate IT governance.

The challenges for IT managers are to co-ordinate and work in partnership with the business to deliver high quality IT services. This has to be achieved while adopting a more business and customer oriented approach to delivering services and cost optimization.

The primary objective of Service Management is to ensure that the IT services are aligned to the business needs and actively support them. It is imperative that the IT services underpin the business processes, but it is also increasingly important that IT acts as an agent for change to facilitate business transformation.
All organizations that use IT depend on IT to be successful. If IT processes and IT services are implemented, managed and supported in the appropriate way, the business will be more successful, suffer less disruption and loss of productive hours, reduce costs, increase revenue, improve public relations and achieve its business objectives.

What is ITIL?

ITIL is a public framework that describes Best Practice in IT service management. It provides a framework for the governance of IT, the 'service wrap', and focuses on the continual measurement and improvement of the quality of IT service delivered, from both a business and a customer perspective. This focus is a major factor in ITIL's worldwide success and has contributed to its prolific usage and to the key benefits obtained by those organizations deploying the techniques and processes throughout their organizations. Some of these benefits include:

- Increased user and customer satisfaction with IT services
- Improved service availability, directly leading to Increased business profits and revenue
- Financial savings from reduced rework, lost time, Improved resource management and usage
- Improved time to market for new products and services
- Improved decision making and optimized risk.

ITIL was published between 1989 and 1995 by Her Majesty's Stationery Office (HMSO) in the UK on behalf of the Central Communications and Telecommunications

Agency (CCTA) – now subsumed within the Office of Government Commerce (OGC). Its early use was principally confined to the UK and Netherlands. A second version of ITIL was published as a set of
revised books between 2000 and 2004. The initial version of ITIL consisted of a library of 31 associated books covering all aspects of IT service provision. This initial version was then revised and replaced by seven, more closely connected and consistent books (ITIL V2) consolidated within an overall framework. This second version became universally accepted and is now used in many countries by thousands of organizations as the basis for effective IT service provision. In 2007, ITIL V2 was superseded by an enhanced and consolidated third version of ITIL, consisting of five core books covering the service lifecycle, together with the official Introduction.

Consider CobiT

For many enterprises, information and the technology that supports it represent their most valuable, but often least understood, assets. Successful enterprises recognize the benefits of information technology and use it to drive their stakeholders' value. These enterprises also understand and manage the associated risks, such as increasing regulatory compliance and critical dependence of many business processes on information technology.

The need for assurance about the value of IT, the management of IT-related risks and increased requirements for control over information are now understood as key elements of enterprise governance. Value, risk and control constitute the core of IT governance. IT governance is the responsibility of executives and the board of directors, and consists of the leadership, organizational structures and processes that ensure that the enterprise's IT sustains and extends the organization's strategies and objectives.

Furthermore, IT governance integrates and institutionalizes good practices to ensure that the enterprise's IT supports the business objectives. IT governance enables the enterprise to take full advantage of its information, thereby maximizing benefits, capitalizing on opportunities and gaining competitive advantage. These outcomes require a framework for control over IT that fits with and supports the Committee of Sponsoring Organizations of the Treadway Commission's (COSO's) Internal Control—Integrated Framework, the widely accepted control framework for enterprise governance and risk management, and similar compliant frameworks.

Organizations should satisfy the quality, fiduciary and security requirements for their information, as for all assets. Management should also optimize the use of available IT resources, including applications, information, infrastructure and people. To discharge these responsibilities, as well as to achieve its objectives, management should understand the status of its enterprise architecture for IT and decide what governance and control it should provide.

Control Objectives for Information and related Technology (COBIT®) provides good practices across a domain and process framework and presents activities in a manageable and logical structure. COBIT's good practices represent the consensus of experts. They are strongly focused more on control, and less on execution. These practices help optimize IT-enabled investments, ensure service delivery and provide a measure against which to judge when things do go wrong.

For IT to be successful in delivering against business requirements, management should put an internal control system or framework in place. The COBIT control framework contributes to these needs by:

• Making a link to the business requirements

• Organizing IT activities into generally accepted process model

• Identifying the major IT resources to be leveraged

• Defining the management control objectives to be considered

The business orientation of COBIT consists of linking business goals to IT goals, providing metrics and maturity models to measure their achievement, and identifying the associated responsibilities of business and IT process owners. The process focus of COBIT is illustrated by a process model that subdivides IT into four domains and 34 processes in line with the responsibility areas of plan, build, run and monitor, providing an end-to-end view of IT. Enterprise architecture concepts help identify the resources essential for process success, i.e., applications, information, infrastructure and people. In summary, to provide the information that the enterprise needs to achieve its objectives, IT resources need to be managed by a set of naturally grouped processes.

But how does the enterprise get IT under control such that it delivers the information the enterprise needs? How does it manage the risks and secure the IT resources on which it is so dependent? How does the enterprise ensure that IT achieves its objectives and supports the business?

First, management needs control objectives that define the ultimate goal of implementing policies, plans and procedures, and organizational structures designed to provide reasonable assurance that:

• Business objectives are achieved

• Undesired events are prevented or detected and corrected

Second, in today's complex environments, management is continuously searching for condensed and timely information to make difficult decisions on value, risk and control quickly and successfully. What should be measured, and how? Enterprises need an objective measure of where they are and where improvement is required, and they need to implement a management tool kit to monitor this improvement. CobiT is that framework!

COBIT Frequently Asked Questions

1. What is the purpose of COBIT?

The purpose of COBIT is to provide management and business process owners with an information technology (IT) governance model that helps in delivering value from IT and understanding and managing the risks associated with IT.

COBIT helps bridge the gaps amongst business requirements, control needs and technical issues.

It is a control model to meet the needs of IT governance and ensure the integrity of information and information systems.

2. Who is using COBIT?

COBIT is used globally by those who have the primary responsibilities for business processes and technology, those who depend on technology for relevant and reliable information, and those providing quality, reliability and control of information technology.

3. Who are the process owners?

COBIT is IT process-oriented and, therefore, addresses itself in the first place to the owners of these processes. Referring to Porter's Generic Business Model, core processes (e.g., procurement, operations, marketing, sales) are discussed, as well as support processes (e.g., human resources, administration, information technology).

As a consequence, COBIT is not only to be applied by the IT department, but by the business as a whole.

This approach stems from the fact that in today's enterprises, the process owners are responsible for the performance of their processes, of which IT has become an integral part. In other words, they are empowered but also accountable. As a consequence, business process owners bear the final responsibility for the information technology as deployed within the confines of their business process. Of course, they will make use of services provided by specialized parties such as the traditional IT department or the third-party service provider.

COBIT provides business process owners with a framework, which should enable them to control all the different activities underlying IT deployment. As a result, on this basis they can gain reasonable assurance that IT will contribute to the achievement of their business objectives. Moreover, COBIT provides business process owners with a generic communication framework to facilitate understanding and clarity amongst the different parties involved in the delivery of IT services.

Furthermore, the management guidelines provide management with a set of tools that allow self-assessment to help make choices for control implementation and improvements over IT, and measure the achievement of goals and the proper performance of IT processes. The management guidelines include maturity models; key goals and metrics; and responsible, accountable, consulted and/or informed (RACI) charts to clarify roles and responsibilities to support managerial decision making.

4. Why was the orientation of COBIT focused on the process rather than functions or applications?

The COBIT framework has been structured into 34 IT processes clustering interrelated life cycle activities or interrelated discrete tasks.

The process model was preferred for several reasons. First, a process by its nature is results-oriented in the way that it focuses on the final outcome while optimizing the use of resources.

The way these resources are physically structured, e.g., people/skills in departments, is less relevant in this perspective.

Second, a process, especially its objectives, is more permanent in nature and does not risk change as often as an organizational   entity.

Third, the deployment of IT cannot be confined to a particular department and involves users and management as well as IT specialists. In this context, the IT process remains, nevertheless, the common denominator.

As far as applications are concerned, they are treated within the COBIT framework as one of the four resource categories. Hence they are to be managed and controlled in such a way as to bring about the required information at the business process level. This way, application systems are an integral part of the COBIT framework and can be addressed specifically through the resource vantage point. In other words, focusing strictly on the resources only, one would automatically get an application view of the COBIT objectives.

5. How robust are the business requirements?

During the review process of COBIT, senior managers and CIOs liked the definition of the business requirements for information, and supported the choices about which requirements were most important in what process. Choices were difficult and entailed considerable debate among the experts during the project. The guiding principle has always been: What really is fundamental for this control objective in this process? Which resource needs special control? Which information requirement needs special attention?

With the development of COBIT 4.1, the understanding of business requirements has been strengthened by the addition of generic business goals and a business-goal-to-IT-goal-to-IT-process cascade. These generic goals, based on extensive industry research, help COBIT users align their business requirements with specific critical processes.

6. What is the overall quality of COBIT, and were any process owners/executives part of the expert review? To assure the high level of quality of COBIT, several measures have been taken. The most important are:

•The whole research process has been overseen by the IT Governance Committee (ITGC), which is responsible for all ITGI research, and directed by the COBIT Steering Committee (CSC). Besides preconceiving the deliverables, the CSC has also been responsible for the final quality of these deliverables.
•A CIO panel provides insights and suggestions for further developments.
•The detailed research results have been quality-controlled throughout.
•The preliminary research involved several COBIT development groups based around the world.

•Before being issued, the final texts were distributed to more than 100 specialists, including process owners, business managers and analysts, such as Gartner, to obtain their comments.

Overall, experience shows that the COBIT model appeals to members of business management as a whole; they appreciate the added value of it in view of improving their control over IT. In this regard, ITGI is confident that the required quality level, beyond customer satisfaction, has been achieved, although feedback is always welcomed and considered. Because COBIT development is a continuous improvement process based on real experience by users, there will always be potential improvements to quality and usefulness.

7. What is the future direction of COBIT?

As with any comprehensive and groundbreaking research, COBIT will be updated to a new version approximately every three years, with minor enhancements in between.

This will ensure that the model and the framework remain comprehensive and valid. The validation will also entail ensuring that the primary reference materials have not changed, or, if they have, those changes are reflected in the document.

8. How did ISACA/ITGI decide on the list of primary references?

The list of primary references was developed as a collective consensus based on the experience of the professionals who participated in the CSC's research, expert review and quality assurance efforts.

9. Can I use COBIT as a statement of criteria for specific audit conclusions?

Yes, basing the IT Assurance Guide firmly on the control objectives takes the auditor's opinion out of the audit conclusion, replacing it with authoritative criteria. COBIT is based on more than 40 standards and best practices documents for information technology from standards-setting bodies (public and private) worldwide. These include documents from Europe, Canada, Australia, Japan and the United States. Because COBIT contains all pertinent worldwide standards identifiable at the time of publication, it is all-inclusive with respect to IT controls standards. As a result, COBIT can be used as an authoritative source reference document, providing IT controls criteria on audits.

10. Are the control objectives meant to be a minimum level of control or best practice?

IT control objectives are statements of managerial actions to achieve necessary outcomes or purposes to control risk and add value within a particular IT process. They are written as short, action-oriented management practices and expressed wherever possible in a life cycle sequence. Control objectives are complemented by COBIT Control Practices, Guidance to Achieve Control Objectives for Successful IT Governance, 2nd Edition, which describe a set of management actions designed to attain the outcomes described in the control objective.

Management makes choices relative to control objectives:

•Selecting those that are applicable in the enterprise's setting
•Determining the cost-benefit ratio of adopting the control objective, including acceptance of the risk of not implementing a control objective

•Deciding on the actual control practices and implementing them or choosing alternative management actions to achieve the similar outcomes

•Choosing how to implement (frequency, span, resourcing, automation, etc.)

11. What about the absence of platform-specific controls?

The COBIT control objectives are generic in nature and address activities or tasks within IT processes. This way they are platform-independent. However, they are the overall structure wherein more specific platform-related controls are to be defined. In fact, the general control objectives should remain valid regardless of whether one is controlling, for example, a mainframe platform or an office automation platform. It is obvious that certain aspects will require more emphasis in a given environment.

12. Where are the application controls?

The application controls were originally fully integrated in the COBIT model. This option had been taken considering that COBIT is business-process-oriented and that at this level application controls are merely part of the overall controls to be exercised over information systems and related technology. In most cases, however, this part cannot be outsourced. Hence, the question is of prime importance.

Before the publication of COBIT 4.0, there was one process, Manage data, where the traditional transactions and file controls could be found. In COBIT 4.0 the application controls were taken out of DS10 and made part of the COBIT framework using the ACn prefix, because it was decided that they had become accepted as being owned by business process owners and not part of an IT process. With COBIT 4.1, they have been simplified to six key application control objectives, AC1 to 6.

13. Why is there overlap within the control objectives?

Overlap in the control objectives, although not occurring often, was intentional. Some control objectives transcend domains and processes and, therefore, must be repeated to ensure that they exist in each domain or process. Some control objectives are meant to be cross-checks of one another and, therefore, must be repeated to ensure consistent application in more than one domain or process. Thus, although potentially perceived as overlapping, COBIT intentionally repeats some control objectives to ensure appropriate coverage of these IT controls.

14. Are the control objectives linked to the IT Assurance Guide and to what degree?

Objectives have been developed from a process orientation because management is looking for proactive advice on how to address the issue of keeping IT under control.

185

Balancing cost and risk is the next issue to address (i.e., making a conscious choice of how and whether to implement each control objective). The link is the process. The control objectives help management establish control over the process. The IT Assurance Guide testing steps assist the auditor or assessor by providing assurance that the process is actually under control, such that the information requirements necessary to achieve business objectives will be satisfied.

In reference to the control framework represented by the waterfall model, the testing steps can be seen as providing the feedback from the control processes back to the business objectives. The control objectives are the guide going down the waterfall to get the IT process under control. The IT Assurance Guide testing steps are the guide for going back up the waterfall with the question: 'Is there assurance that the business objective will be achieved?' The 2007 IT Assurance Guide provides specific tests at the process and control objective level, whereas the previous Audit Guidelines provided tests at only the process level.

15. Why are there no risk statements with the control objectives?

The provision of risk statements was seriously considered and investigated during the research and review phase of the initial COBIT project, but not retained because management preferred the proactive approach (objects are to be achieved) over the reactive approach (risks are to be mitigated).

The risk approach comes in at the end of the IT Assurance Guide when the risk of not implementing the controls is substantiated. In the application of COBIT, the risk approach is certainly useful when management decides which controls to implement or when auditors decide which control objectives to review. Both of these decisions depend entirely on the risk environment.

In the management guidelines the goals and metrics can be used as risk indicators by considering their absence or lack of positive outcomes. Also, the control practices provide risk and value statements at the control objective level, indicating the risks of not implementing a control objective and the value of improving the control.

16. What training is available for the use of COBIT?

ISACA has developed and is continually enhancing its education and training portfolio supporting COBIT. Currently the portfolio consists of:

-Internet-based self-paced modules;

http://cobitcampus3.isaca.org/isaca/Catalog/index.aspx, covering:

-COBIT Awareness Course™

-COBIT Foundation Course™ (with an associated COBIT Foundation Examination™)

-COBIT for Sarbanes-Oxley Compliance™

-Classroom-based course,
http://cobitcampus3.isaca.org/isaca/index.aspx, covering:

-Implementing IT Governance using COBIT™

17. Who in my organization should go to the training?

COBIT training should be attended by management, IS and audit managers, IT professionals, business process managers, and quality assurance and audit professionals.

18. What is the level of training required?

The amount and level of training necessary is a function of how comfortable one feels with the product; however, practical experience has shown that successful implementation is directly related to the amount of COBIT knowledge acquired. Therefore, training is considered to be very important but the training also has to be properly and correctly provided, which is why ISACA developed a portfolio of courses. The IT Governance Implementation Guide: Using COBIT and Val IT, 2nd Edition, and the IT Assurance Guide provide valuable support following attendance at training courses.

19. In what way can I suggest to IT management that it use COBIT?

Because COBIT is business-oriented, using it to understand IT control objectives to deliver IT value and manage IT-related business risks is straightforward:

1. Start with business objectives in the framework.

2. Select the IT processes and control objectives appropriate to the enterprise from the control objectives.

3. Operate from the business plan.

4. Assess the status of the organization, identify critical activities leading to success and measure performance in reaching enterprise goals with the management guidelines.

5. Assess procedures and results with the IT Assurance Guide.

20. Is the COBIT framework superior to the other accepted control models?

Most senior managers are aware of the importance of the general control frameworks with respect to their fiduciary responsibility, such as COSO, Cadbury, CoCo or King II; however, they may not necessarily be aware of the details of each. In addition, management is increasingly aware of the more technical security guidance such as ISO 17799, and service delivery guidance such as ITIL. Although the aforementioned models emphasize business control and IT security and service issues, only COBIT attempts to deal with IT-specific control issues from a business perspective. It should be noted that COSO was used as source material for the business model and ISO 17799 and ITIL, amongst many others, were used to develop the control objectives. COBIT is not meant to replace any of these control models. It is intended to emphasize what control is required in the IT environment while working with and building on the strengths of these other control models.

21. What is the quickest and best way to sell COBIT to IT managers?

As we all know, there is no cavalry to come to the rescue. As the rest of the implementation tools point out, the organizational culture is vitally important. A proactive culture will be more receptive than one that is not. However, consider emphasizing the business aspects and the fact that COBIT does not get lost in technical terminology.

Furthermore, point out that COBIT was designed the way an IT manager thinks, and one of its greatest benefits is that everything is documented in one place.

With the addition of the management guidelines, COBIT provides management with new capabilities to support self-assessment of organizational status, comparison with industry good practices, alignment with enterprise objectives, implementation decision making and performance monitoring. The maturity models, key goal indicators and key performance indicators provided in these guidelines can assist management in better aligning IT with the overall enterprise strategy by ensuring that IT is an enabler of the enterprise goals.

22. Since COBIT currently does not address associated business risks, but rather the more proactive control statements to be achieved, is there any consideration being given to address the perceived need of risk identification?

Risk is addressed in a pervasive manner throughout COBIT and even more so with the advent of the management guidelines. A major driver of the control and assurance processes is the IT governance model that is now covered extensively in COBIT and the management guidelines framework.

IT governance refers to the generic enterprise objectives of measuring benefits and managing risk. The same idea, risk management as an enterprise objective, was nevertheless already captured by COBIT earlier, because COBIT states that IT needs to provide information to the enterprise that must have the required characteristics to enable the achievement of enterprise objectives. While the security-related criteria of availability, integrity and confidentiality may be more readily associated with risk, not achieving enterprise objectives or not providing the required criteria is a risk that the enterprise needs to control.

Specific examples have been provided in the 'substantiating' section of the IT Assurance Guide. The objective of that section is to document for management what can or has happened as a result of not having effective control in place. More practically, one entire process was defined to cover the assessment of risk. (See PO9 Assess and manage IT risks.)

Risk is addressed in the framework in a proactive manner, i.e., by focusing on objectives, because the primary risk that needs to be managed is that of not achieving the objectives. The section on documenting the impact of control weaknesses of the IT Assurance Guide provides examples of these risks for each process. This provides for the risk information for which the control and assurance professional is looking. A whole IT process is dedicated to the assessment of risk in the overall set of IT objectives.

23. Has the COBIT framework been accepted by CIOs?

Yes, it has been accepted in many organizations globally, and new cases continue to be documented. However, it should not surprise anyone that in those entities where the CIO has embraced COBIT as a usable IT framework, this has come as a direct consequence of one or more COBIT champions within the audit and/or IT department(s).

Even more important than acceptance by the CIO is acceptance by the board and executive management. Successful implementation of IT governance using COBIT depends greatly on the commitment of top management.

The addition of the management guidelines should also increase the acceptance of COBIT by enterprise and IT management. The emphasis on alignment of IT with enterprise goals, self-assessment and performance measurement will ensure that COBIT is seen not only as a control framework, but also as providing a set of tools for improving the effectiveness of information and IT resources. The integration of the management guidelines with the COBIT framework and control objectives provide additional emphasis for management to use COBIT as the authoritative, up-to-date and established model for IT control and governance.

24. How are the management guidelines integrated into the COBIT framework?

Starting with the COBIT framework, the application of international standards and guidelines and research into good practices led to the development of the control objectives. Management needed a similar application of the framework to allow self-assessment and choices to be made for control implementation and improvements over its information and related technology.

The management guidelines provide the tools to accomplish this. They were developed for each of the 34 IT processes, with a management and performance measurement perspective. Maturity models, goals and metrics, and roles and responsibilities (RACI) charts are provided by the guidelines to support management decision-making processes.

With COBIT 4.0 the management guidelines were integrated and positioned together with the control objectives in one complete publication, to give users a single complete source.

25. The COBIT framework states that the COBIT maturity

models are derived from the SEI Capability Maturity Model (CMM). What is the actual relationship between COBIT and CMM?

The maturity models (MMs) in COBIT were first created in 2000 and at that time were designed based on the original CMM scale with the addition of an extra level (0) as shown below:
Level 0: Non-existent
Level 1: Initial/ad hoc
Level 2: Repeatable but Intuitive
Level 3: Defined Process
Level 4: Managed and Measurable
Level 5: optimized

The use of this scale is the only relationship to CMM, as it was felt that the CMM approach, designed for rigorous software development environments, was not appropriate for COBIT where the approach is at a strategic level and focused on high-level IT management processes.

The purpose of the COBIT MMs is to provide a management tool enabling benchmarking and targeting of desired process maturity levels and to encourage process improvement via gap analysis. Although concepts of the CMM approach were followed, the COBIT implementation differs considerably from the original CMM, which was oriented toward software product engineering principles, organizations striving for excellence in these areas and formal appraisal of maturity levels so that software developers could be 'certified'.

A generic definition was created for the COBIT MM scale, which is similar to CMM but interpreted for the nature of COBIT's processes. A specific model was then developed from this generic scale for each of COBIT's 34 processes. A maturity attribute generic scale was also developed, using six attributes. This scale was not based on any CMM concepts but was created by the COBIT expert development team.

Since 2000, the COBIT MMs and maturity attributes have been refined and adjusted based on experience and feedback. The SEI discontinued the original CMM and replaced it with a new model called CMMI. CMMI has not been used in the development of the COBIT MMs.

26. Do I need to meet an exact level when assessing a process using COBIT's maturity models, and does this differ from the original CMM approach?

The main purpose of the COBIT maturity models is to give management a tool to help them better understand the current capability of IT management processes, do benchmarking, gap analysis and improvement planning.

With COBIT's maturity models, unlike the original SEI CMM approach, there is no intention to measure levels precisely or try to certify that a level has exactly been met. It is also not strictly true in COBIT that a lower level must be fully complied with before higher levels of maturity can be reached, as in CMM. A COBIT maturity assessment is likely to result in a profile where conditions relevant to several maturity levels will be met.

This is because when assessing maturity is often the case that some implementation is in place at different levels even if it is not complete or sufficient. These strengths can be built on to further improve maturity. For example, some parts of the process can be well defined and, even if the process is incomplete, it would be misleading to say the process is not defined at all.

Furthermore, if the six generic maturity attributes defined in COBIT are also assessed to give a more detailed analysis, it is quite likely that each attribute may be at a different level, too (e.g., policies, standards and procedures may be defined, but goal setting and measurement may be ad hoc).

It is, therefore, best to choose a level based on the 'closest fit', while appreciating and understanding the positive things that have been implemented as well as the gaps that need to be improved. In the example, the process would be said to be at level 3. It would also be misleading and imply an unreal level of precision to describe the process as being at, say, level 2.9.

In COBIT the important objective is to understand what level is appropriate for a given process, based on business requirements, and to understand the nature of any gaps, so that any significant weaknesses in the process can be identified and improved. Guidance on this approach is provided in the IT Governance Implementation Guide: Using COBIT and Val IT, 2nd Edition.

27. COBIT has three dimensions of maturity. What do they mean?

The three dimensions, as explained in the COBIT framework, are capability, performance and control. They can be used to be more precise when assessing maturity for a given IT process in a specific situation. The application of these dimensions is left to the COBIT user to decide depending on how detailed and precise the maturity assessment needs to be and the scope of the assessment target area.

Capability is the level of maturity required in the process to meet business requirements (ideally driven by clearly defined business and IT goals). The COBIT maturity models focus on capability and help an enterprise recognise the capability that best fits specific process requirements.

Coverage is a measure of performance, i.e., how and where the capability needs to be deployed based on business need, and investment decisions based on costs and benefits. For example, a high level of security may have to be focused upon only for the most critical enterprise systems.

Control is a measure of actual control and execution of the process, in managing risks and delivering the value expected in line with business requirements and risk appetite.

A process may appear to be at the right capability level with the right management characteristics, but still fail because of an inadequate control design. This is an assessment against the COBIT control objectives considered necessary for the process. COBIT provides a generic maturity model for internal control, and processes PO6 and ME2 help institutionalize the need for good controls.

Given the above, it is possible to use all of these dimensions to carry out a detailed assessment of maturity for a specific critical area, for example, security of a banking application, or the overall change management process. At a high level they can also be used to provide an overall and thorough assessment of the maturity of a process by considering all three dimensions in the context of the overall business requirement.

28. How do you perform a COBIT-based maturity assessment?

The reality is that probably no two COBIT maturity assessments are performed in exactly the same manner. COBIT provides some tools and techniques, and the COBIT user will follow an approach based on specific enterprise needs. The assessments can be high-level, often in a workshop discussion, or detailed with careful gap analysis.

Generically, the following common principles usually apply:
•The maturity requirements should be driven by business requirements ideally expressed as business and IT goals.
•The requirements depend on the scope being considered and can be very specific for a particular scope or high-level if the scope is for the enterprise as a whole.
•The maturity models help assess capability (defined in COBIT to mean how well the process is being managed in comparison to the COBIT maturity models and attributes).
•The maturity attributes can be used to analyze current maturity levels in detail and are required to do a proper gap analysis.
•COBIT's control objectives provide a way to measure how well the process addresses key controls needed to minimize risk and deliver value.

•COBIT's control practices can be used to help design improved processes and to increase process maturity, together with other industry standards and best practices.

It is recommended that that the maturity attributes be used to assess at a detailed level and to carry out a gap analysis, so that the root causes of immaturity can be identified and business decisions can be taken on where to invest to improve maturity for least cost and maximum benefit. IT Governance Implementation Guide: Using COBIT and Val IT, 2nd Edition, provides a road map that includes guidance on the above steps.

29. How prescriptive are the COBIT maturity models and supporting guidance, and how does this compare to the CMM/CMMI approach?

The MMs in COBIT, like all the COBIT guidance, are intended to be tailored and developed to suit the specific needs of the enterprise. The guidance is also at a high level with the intention that it provides generic guidance, not specific, detailed criteria. In particular, the maturity attributes are very generic and high-level, intended to be a simple guide for any process. When performing a COBIT maturity assessment, specific attribute details will need to be identified for the process under review, and compared to COBIT's control objectives, control practices, and goals and metrics to the desired level of detail. COBIT does not prescribe the assessment approach, which is a management decision, ranging from a high-level workshop discussion to an in-depth analysis, as appropriate, driven by business needs.

In CMM/CMMI, although the guidance would always need to be tailored for a given appraisal situation, the standard guidance is much more specific and detailed, due to its much narrower focus on software product delivery and more formal appraisal/assessment procedure.

30. The CMMI maturity levels appear to be different to the COBIT maturity levels. Is this true?

Yes, CMMI uses the following scale:

Level 0: Incomplete
Level 1: Performed
Level 2: Managed
Level 3: Defined
Level 4: Quantitatively Managed
Level 5: Optimising

COBIT's scale differs:

Level 0: Non-existent
Level 1: Initial/ad hoc
Level 2: Repeatable but Intuitive
Level 3: Defined Process
Level 4: Managed and Measurable
Level 5: optimized

There is no direct relationship between these two scales. The COBIT scale was based on the original CMM scale and has remained the same since the first version of the COBIT maturity models were released in 2000. There was never any intention to align the models exactly with CMM or CMMI when it was introduced, or to try to maintain any such alignment, as COBIT's maturity modeling approach is based on different objectives to the Software Engineering Institute's (SEI's) objectives.

COBIT's models provide management with a self-assessment tool for positioning IT process capability in comparison to business requirements, and as a tool for gap analysis and improvement planning, taking into account the required capability driven by business requirements (business and IT goals), control requirements (control objectives) and performance (how much and where to implement, driven by costs and benefits).

CMMI provides a rigorous, objective and repeatable assessment, and fulfils the needs of organizations requiring certifications to meet contractual needs, or needing to demonstrate development engineering capabilities of a high maturity for customers where software development is critical.

31. Is it really possible to benchmark my maturity levels with other organizations if the maturity assessments are not very precisely measured?

Yes, even though COBIT's maturity levels are not intended to be measured precisely, the levels give a good guide to management. Even when an approximate assessment is carried out, for example, in a management workshop, the level selected is usually a sound reflection of the actual level. Benchmark comparisons provided in COBIT Online from user input and from surveys are helpful to managers for comparing their organization to others.

The data collected have also empirically validated the broad nature of the actual measures there are few 'unusual' scores, IT processes even in large and significant enterprises are generally not well developed in most IT functions, and most organizations have COBIT-defined process maturity that is relatively low, i.e., between levels 2 and 3.

32. Are COBIT's maturity models useful to organizations that have already adopted CMMI?

Yes, even though the approaches are different, an enterprise that has already adopted and applied CMMI can use COBIT to cover areas not addressed by CMMI, and will be able to use the CMMI experience to apply COBIT's models to whatever formal level they require, in areas not covered by the scope that was defined for the CMMI assessment.
For example, an advanced software development shop could broaden its maturity assessment to apply it to their entire IT function, including other important COBIT IT processes. The mapping publication, available from the ITGI, showing how COBIT compares to CMMI, would be a very helpful resource, but the enterprise would need to devise its own CMMI-like assessment approach using COBIT's generic guidance as a starting point, or follow the suggested approach in the ITGI publication—IT Governance

Implementation Guide: Using COBIT and Val IT, 2nd Edition. In time, it is expected that the CMMI guidance will broaden into other areas such as service management, which would be equivalent to the ITIL processes and principally the COBIT DS domain.

Formal Risk Management

Risk is a business issue. Issues arise when businesses take it for granted that risk management is solely an IT concern. This disconnect can actually increase risk, rather than mitigate it. It is therefore imperative for IT leaders to communicate to executives the importance of coordinated risk management.

The Importance of Risk Management

New direction from regulators such as the Securities and Exchange Commission (SEC) and the PCAOB are urging enterprises to focus their IT efforts on high-risk areas relative to their own environments. In other words, SOX initiatives will evolve to include customized compliance, as opposed to adherence to rigid, inflexible auditing standards (such as the PCAOB's Auditing Standard No. 2). Typically, a proper risk management portfolio includes the following elements:

Purpose of Risk Assessment	Trigger/Business Driver	Benefit
Compliance initiative	Legislation, annual audits	Positive audit results
Identify unknown risks	Business continuity goals	Formal list of risks
Minimize risk issues	Corporate mandate	Demonstrate savings
Meet stakeholder needs	Reporting requirements	Increased value

Furthermore, IT security and compliance are merging under the risk management umbrella due to market forces such as multiple legislative requirements, increasing numbers of malicious attacks, and the need to manage corporate governance and IT/business alignment.

As these forces converge, enterprises scramble to fulfill numerous requirements without much forethought, the result of which is conflicting duties and lack of true ownership.

- **The CFO** is tasked with risk management because he or she has intimate knowledge of financial reporting and fiscal responsibility. Gaps can form, for example, in cases where legislative compliance has a strong IT security angle, yet the CFO is not well-versed in risk issues specific to IT.
- **The CSO** is tasked with risk management, but this individual is technically-oriented and therefore has minimal knowledge of business issues. The result is too strong a focus on IT security, and not enough on business risk.
- **The CIO** is tasked with risk management, compliance, and security because the business assumes that these three issues are IT problems alone. The CIO ends up working in a vacuum without any direction or advice on how to manage risk.

Types of Risk

There is more at risk, of course, than just government-mandated legislation. Other areas of risk include business continuity, technology adoption, security issues, quality of policies or procedures, etc. Major and minor risks to all aspects of the enterprise must be evaluated and assessed. IT must therefore analyze risks that the business faces outside of the typical data center environment:

External Risks	**Internal Risks**
• Fire	• Equipment failure
• Power outages	• IT and physical security breaches
• Flooding	• Sabotage
• Civil unrest (war, local instability)	• Labor disputes, staff turnover
• Terrorism	• Interruption of communications
• Consumer confidence	• Interruption of computer services
• Storms (hurricane, blizzard, etc.)	• Fraud

Then, of course, there are the costs of risks should they become realized. Some aspects of costs are very easy to calculate, while others are more complicated. Cost factors are usually broken down into two distinct categories: Financial and Goodwill. Financial Cost Factors are measured in dollars, while Goodwill Cost Factors are an intangible measured in relative impact on the enterprise. The following is a list of potential cost factors associated with realized risk:

Financial Cost Factors	**Goodwill Cost Factors**
• Loss of revenue	• Production delays
• Loss of productivity	• Loss of consumer confidence
• Increased cost of sales	• Loss of company reputation
• Increased operating costs	• Decline in customer service
• Increased labor costs	
• Remediation costs	
• Loss of efficiency	
• Legal costs (e.g. compliance fines)	

Establishing the Need for Risk Management

The role of risk management is to balance varying levels of risk against the cost of mitigating those risks. As such, the enterprise needs strategic, tactical, operational, and technical capability. To determine the need for formal risk management, complete the checklist below, as per corporate requirements.

Answering "yes" to nine or more of the requirements below means that the enterprise needs a dedicated and formal risk management. Answering "yes" to between five and eight requirements indicates that the enterprise should bestow risk management duties on either the CIO or CFO. Answering "yes" to four or less indicates relatively minor need, and means that risk management duties may be distributed even further, as appropriate.

Requirements

- Does the enterprise need or require oversight of information security and compliance risks?

- Does the enterprise need or require a person to identify risks and the IT solutions, policies, or processes that will mitigate risk?

- Does the enterprise need a company-wide corporate security policy that meets company goals and objectives, and maps to critical IT functions?

- Is there adequate communication between business leaders, executive team, project managers, and other stakeholders on all things risk-related?

- Does the enterprise need or require a corporate strategy for IT security, architecture, and compliance Initiatives?

- Does the enterprise need or require the use of standardized risk assessment models or frameworks, as well as procedures for monitoring, measuring, and reporting the enterprise's risk and security posture?

- Are accountability and transparency into internal controls used to achieve compliance and mitigate risk?

- Does the enterprise conduct regular audit reviews, including projects for corrective actions as prescribed by internal and external auditors?

- Does the enterprise need or require a data classification program to determine the value of corporate information assets, the risks to those assets, and mitigating controls that protect the assets?

- Does the enterprise need or require a program in place for keeping executive management informed and advised on new developments in the regulatory space, as they relate to IT?

- Does the enterprise need or require a risk management function that will provide input to business continuity and disaster recovery plans?

- Does anyone review procedures for day-to-day management of IT security operations?

- Does the enterprise need to permit security and compliance awareness training programs for all relevant staff?

Recommendations

1. **Communicate questionnaire results.** The first step is to take the results of the questions above and communicate them to senior management. This will help put across the idea that the enterprise needs to take greater steps toward improving risk management processes such as risk assessments (quarterly or annually), project planning, and regular updates.

2. **Determine executive commitment to risk management.** From a risk management perspective, aligning IT with the business is crucial. One way to do this is to demonstrate the ROI of security investments, DRP, and other areas where risk plays a strong role in IT operations. Lack of alignment is a very real concern. According to a survey conducted by Pricewaterhouse Coopers of 717 audit managers conducting multiple risk assessments;
   - 20% of companies consider their risk management "well aligned."
   - 50% of companies consider their risk management "somewhat aligned."
   - 30% of companies consider their risk management "not well aligned."
3. **Coordinate efforts with other risk management champions.** Internal audit exists to communicate what type of risk exposures exist within the enterprise. Where there are internal audit teams, create and leverage IT's relationship with them. As more groups become involved in enterprise risk management, coordination and communication become even more crucial. While collaboration is a good thing, it can also lead to confusion caused by overlapping duties, poor communication, and lack of concerted direction or focus.
4. **Align projects with the greatest areas of risk.** Assign ownership to the right person or function. For example, the Pricewaterhouse study found that only 31% of audit/risk management functions reporting directly to a committee or CEO devoted more than 50% of their time on Sarbanes-Oxley compliance. By contrast, 69% of audit/risk management functions reporting to a lower-level role such as controller spent more than 50% of their time on SOX compliance. These findings demonstrate the importance of assigning risk ownership to the appropriate body.

In Summary

In instances where the business is unable or unwilling to assume responsibility for risk management, it is often left to the CIO or IT director to shoulder the burden. Tackle the enterprise's risk portfolio using a sound understanding of the business issues at hand.

Is Constant Help Desk Turnover Good?

On average, enterprises are spending more than 70% of their help desk budget on staffing, with almost half of the staff allocated to first response tier one support positions. With staffing being a large part of the help desk budget, it is important to analyze the impact that employee turnover and tenure has on help desk efficiency.

Help Desk Staffing Profile Percentages:

Tier 1 Support = 49%
Tier 2 Support = 26%
Management = 12%
Tier 3 Support = 10%
Queue Managers = 3%

Looking at Help Desk Turnover

Despite common beliefs that turnover is high in help desk positions, recent research reveals that this is not always true. Organizational turnover was higher than help desk turnover in companies surveyed.

Further analysis reveals that, in some cases, higher turnover among help desk staff may actually improve help desk performance by reinvigorating the support function and cycling in fresh new employees. Conversely, extremely low turnover can be detrimental to the support function. Enterprises with lower than average help desk turnover were found to have the following characteristics:

- **Higher cost per user:** Enterprises with lower turnover were, on average, spending more on their help desk per end user on an annual basis.
- **Lower help desk FTE to end users ratio:** Enterprises with lower turnover had, on average, a

lower number of users being supported per help desk staff.

Looking at Help Desk Tenure

Currently, more than a quarter of all help desk positions are held for over five years.

Help Desk Tenure Averages:

0 – 2 Years = 14%
2 – 5 Years = 59%
5 – 10 Years = 23%
Over 10 Years = 5%

High tenure among help desk staff, particularly tier one support functions, causes the enterprise to pay higher than average salaries for these employees. Enterprises with higher than average help desk tenure were found to have a higher percentage of their budget devoted to staffing costs.

How Low Turnover and High Tenure Increases Costs

While extremely high turnover can be very costly for an organization due to recruiting costs, training and ramp up time, a moderate level of turnover within each help desk position has been shown to be beneficial for the following reasons.

	Low Turnover and High Tenure	High Turnover and Low Tenure
Salaries	When staff stay within a role for longer, their salaries increase year over year and budget for staffing expenses increase as well. Since the bulk of help desk staffing is tier one, considered an entry level IT role, these organizations may be overpaying to staff these positions if staff stay in the role for longer than five yrs.	Enterprises with higher turnover in tier one are able to minimize staffing costs by hiring fresh new talent. These types of employees have also been known to work overtime voluntarily because they are trying to establish themselves within the organization.
Career Progression	Enterprises with higher than average tenure can be a result of limited advancement opportunities. This staff, if kept in the role for more than five years, can be underutilized.	Lower tenure is often due to the promotion of staff to other positions within the IT department. Turnover due to career progression allows key talent to maximize their job potential.
Process Improvements	Enterprises with low turnover and high tenure are more likely to be conservative in their approach to help desk process improvements. Staff with high tenure can be more resistant to process change and the implementation of new tools.	These enterprises are more likely to look for cost savings opportunities and optimize help desk processes. They are more likely to implement tools such as end user self help, knowledge management and asset management, which help to optimize help desk efficiency.

Recommendations

The steps listed below in the order below will reinvigorate the help desk culture, and improve help desk processes:

1. **Balance investment with a realistic tenure expectation.** Give staff the materials and tools that they need to succeed in their job. Provide staff training to help improve their communication, business, and technical skills. Train staff to a level appropriate to their jobs and to advance them, but prepare to move them out before they cost too much.
2. **Properly manage turnover.** Aim for moderate turnover, no more than a 20% yearly turnover rate and a minimum of 2 years of tenure, as extremely high turnover can be costly and eventually affect the reputation of the enterprise. Turnover due to the promotion of employees is positive whereas turnover due to poor hours, management, job responsibilities or company culture should be evaluated and properly managed.
3. **Ensure proper knowledge transfer.** In addition to minimizing orientation costs, the other most commonly cited benefit of low turnover is a more knowledgeable staff. Those with high turnover need defined processes for knowledge transfer and sharing from tenured staff to new staff.
4. **Become more proactive.** Consider implementing end user self service, self help, power users, and automated tools to free up help desk staff time to work on more problem management and change management and less incident management. Giving tier one support staff more proactive job tasks better prepares them for other positions within the IT department.
5. **Assess staff performance.** Formally assessing the performance of staff is correlated to performance. Give help desk staff access to both their efficiency and end-user satisfaction metrics so that they can easily identify self improvement initiatives. Tie their ability to meet these goals to their performance.

In Summary

Experiencing turnover among help desk staff should not always be viewed negatively. Many enterprises with lower help desk tenure are more efficient in serving their end users.

IT Project Success

Many enterprises are plagued with underperforming IT projects. A recent survey explored the differences between successful and unsuccessful projects in terms of product evaluation and selection. Three statistically significant factors emerged. Use these factors as guidelines for reviewing existing processes and for establishing new ones.

Profiling Project Success

The survey collected responses from over 2800 individuals representing organizations of all sizes from a variety of different industries. The respondents provided information on their experiences with major IT projects such as VoIP, Virtualization, ERP, and Business Intelligence (BI). The survey also collected data on the success of these projects in terms of business benefits, competitive advantage, budget, and schedule. These metrics were combined to establish an overall project success score.

In comparing the patterns of product evaluation and implementation of 152 organizations with successful projects to the patterns of 110 organizations with underperforming projects. The analysis revealed three statistically significant differences between successful and unsuccessful IT projects. It also revealed four other heavily weighted factors.

The study revealed a number of heuristics for IT project success.

Differentiating Factors for Successful IT Projects

Differentiators of Successful Projects

Statistically Significant Factors	• Hardware vendor provided input.
Heavily Weighted Factors	• Hardware vendor involved in the project.

Differentiating Factors for Under-Performing IT Projects

Differentiators of Underperforming Projects

Statistically Significant Factors	• Consultants for IT department did not identify potential product/service suppliers. • Senior business management involved in the project.
Heavily Weighted Factors	• Consultants for business management provided input. • Functional management selected the product/service supplier.

Analysis

1. **The consultant.** The involvement of consultants is generally an indication of underperforming projects. This finding should not be interpreted as a call to ban consultants from IT projects. Recognize that consultants have an important role in the success of many projects, particularly ERP projects. Consultants do, however, have an adverse impact

on the cost component of most IT projects. Many managers of smaller IT shops succumb to the siren call of consultants because they lack head count. But consultants are no replacement for a project approach that considers the input of all enterprise stakeholders. A consultant, for example, can't replace the insight on actual work processes provided by end users. Using consultants to identify potential suppliers is a particularly dangerous practice.

2. **Senior business management.** The extent of senior business management involvement has a significant impact on IT project performance. Senior management sponsorship is important, particularly for very large IT departments (500+ full-time staff); but over-involvement of senior management can be disastrous for many IT projects. Final product selection should involve all project stakeholders. This problem is particularly acute with CRM projects. Management's input is particularly crucial in projects such as VoIP and BI. VoIP project success requires senior management support due to its enterprise-wide nature—all employees are affected when the phones go down. BI needs senior management support to establish key reporting objectives and metrics.

3. **The hardware vendor.** Involving the hardware vendor is, in general, a key differentiator for both application (e.g. ERP, BI, CRM) and infrastructure projects (e.g. VoIP). It is, however, inadvisable in virtualization projects where hardware vendors are a risk for defining the product and service needs. Two types of benefits generally emerge from vendor involvement:

    o **Appropriate scoping.** Application projects are notorious for poorly scoped hardware requirements. Involving the hardware vendor provides some guidance on the scalability and reliability issues that application architects may overlook. This problem is particularly acute in BI and ERP projects.

- o **Product families.** Hardware vendors can provide guidance on related solution types. A Storage Area Network (SAN) vendor, for example, can provide guidance on tape backup systems. The ease of integration for these technologies may yield positive project outcomes such as improved on-time performance

Hardware vendor involvement is particularly important for smaller IT firms that may lack the budget to hire or contract skilled resources. Involvement of the hardware vendor becomes more important for project success as IT departments grow from 10 to 100 full-time staff.

Key Takeaways

The analysis points to a number of key questions that managers should use to evaluate their current IT projects. These questions serve as a diagnostic for the most significant project problems. The appropriate response is indicated in parentheses.

1. **Consider the role of consultants.**
   - o Are consultants actually contributing any benefit to the project? (Yes)
   - o Are consultants being used to replace full-time staff for operational tasks? (No)
   - o Are the consultants qualified to perform the anticipated scope of work as demonstrated by industry certification? (Yes)
   - o Do the consultants have references qualifying their experience in completing the anticipated scope of work? (Yes)
   - o Are consultants being used in an attempt to shortcut a formal requirements gathering process? (No)
2. **Evaluate the role of management.**
   - o Do senior managers carry sole responsibility for product selection? (No)

- Is senior management involved in projects related to core operations such as systems for financial management or business reporting? (Yes)
- Is senior management involved in projects that have a broad impact footprint in the enterprise (e.g. VoIP)? (Yes)
- Is management over-involved in infrastructure projects such as storage consolidation or virtualization? (No)

3. **Include the hardware vendor.**
   - Has the project team consulted with hardware vendors? (Yes)
   - Has the project team clearly defined the hardware requirements for the project? (Yes)
   - Does the project team have confidence in the accuracy and validity of the hardware requirements? (Yes)
   - Has the project team determined if there are suitable options within the product families of current technology providers? (Yes)

In Summary

Research reveals three key factors that differentiate IT project success from project failure. Don't let consultants drive IT projects, and include hardware vendors in the evaluation and selection process. Involving senior management in gritty IT details also has a negative impact on projects.

IT Service Quality Improves with Human Sigma

For IT departments demonstrating value is a constant priority. As a service oriented unit of the organization, IT is appraised on the level of service provided to internal and external clients. Service quality, however, is not easily measured. For example, ITIL defined KPIs for successful incident management include mean time incident resolution and total cost per incident. While these are important measurements in evaluating a successful help desk, these metrics are not sufficient in assessing client perceptions of IT services. To improve IT service quality, IT leaders must look beyond technical functionality to the human side of service.

Help Desk: IT Service in the Trenches

To view how an organization perceives its IT department, turn to the front lines. The help desk is an area of IT that is in constant contact with the end users. End-user perception of IT service translates directly to how much value end users recognize from IT. Improving service quality therefore improves IT value. Extending Gallup's premise to the help desk suggests that while help desk ticket backlog may be down and incident turnaround time is low, the true nature of service can only be measured by surveying end users as well as help desk staff, and that these surveys should include questions relating to the emotional perception of the client IT staff interaction. In other words, it's not how we performed, but how the client feels about our performance that counts.

Measuring Service from Six Sigma to Human Sigma

A recent study in customer service quality by researchers at Gallup has garnered some valuable insight into the relation between service providers and their clients, resulting in recommendations that should be of particular interest to IT organizations supporting help desk and other client facing service units. Developed by Fleming, Coffman, and Harter, Human Sigma is based on a set of customer service studies which apply the quality control principles of Six Sigma to the measurement of client or customer service across a sample of businesses.

- **Six Sigma.** Generally applied to quality assurance in manufacturing, Six Sigma was originally developed by Motorola in the eighties. It is a measure and correct quality control approach resulting in an optimized output of 3.4 defects or less per one million occurrences.
- **Human Sigma.** A service quality assurance method measuring both employee and client engagement through a series of scaled questions. Surveys yield a score that can be graphed on a normal distribution curve with outliers on the curve representing low performers or "service defects." Much like Six Sigma, the goals is to reduce defects in order to reach an optimized level of service.

Emotionally Engaged Help Desk Clients Are Repeat Buyers

In studying Human Sigma researchers measured emotional engagement amongst clients as seen in Table 1. Sited in Gallup's studies is a correlation between clients' emotional engagement and increased client loyalty resulting in repeat client purchases. To frame this reaction in an IT context, client loyalty is demonstrated when end users regularly turn to help desk support instead of going through other informal channels for assistance. On the other hand, poor loyalty resulting in staff avoidance of IT is a sign of poor IT service which lowers the perceived organizational value of IT.

Table 1. Measures of Service Quality

Emotional Engagement Criteria

- **Confidence.** Does the client believe the IT organization will deliver on promises?
- **Integrity.** Do clients feel they are treated with respect by IT?
- **Pride.** Do clients identify positively with IT organization?
- **Passion.** Do IT staff and internal clients take pride in their IT department?

Functional Metrics

- **Quality.** How well did the help desk solve end-user problem?
- **Timeliness.** Amount of help desk tickets outstanding or average turnaround time per request.
- **Overall satisfaction.** Is the end user likely to revisit the help desk?

Recommendations

Gallup's research on the topic of Human Sigma demonstrates the importance of client and employee engagement in improving service quality. IT departments ready to take on a service quality improvement initiative should consider these steps derived from Human Sigma studies:

1. **Measure to optimize.** Measure employee performance AND internal client satisfaction.

   - **Measure locally.** Measure within IT, IT sub-structures, varying geographic locations or project groups to isolate problem areas. Company-wide customer service and employee satisfaction surveys will not help optimize service within IT.

217

- **Measure centrally.** Avoid using data hacked together from various locations. For example, an HR employee survey combined with marketing data on client satisfaction. Both end-user satisfaction and employee engagement should be measured relative to each other for optimal measurement.

2. **Correct locally.** Hold local managers or supervisors accountable for department level of service.

- **Supervisors must take action.** Managers, supervisors, and team leads are directly responsible for the level of their department's employee engagement.
- Where outliers appear in measurement, actions should be taken to return the department to within normal distribution.
- **Train the trainer.** Training for supervisors in the way of courses or brief seminars may be necessary where desired results are not obtained from employees.

3. **Rebuild where necessary.** Where corrective action fails, a more drastic approach may be called for, including replacement of ineffective supervisors and a reconsideration of hiring practices within IT.

In Summary

IT departments can improve service quality by taking a lesson from Gallup's customer service studies on managing Human Sigma which emphasize the value of service perception as much as service utility.

Don't Speak Geek

IT often finds it difficult to communicate with non-IT management who must review, approve and support major IT initiatives. Moreover, IT often fails to achieve full benefit from an information technology investment. When IT explains how to use technology in terms that the users do not understand, users will not use it properly.

What We Have Is a Failure to Communicate Effectively

Communication often fails when IT staff members use technical language that is either not understood by non-technical staff (for example, ITIL) or is ambiguous (such as Web 2.0). To compound the problem, IT brings forward issues in terms that have meaning for IT, but which have little relevance to the business. For example, consider a situation in which IT proposes to invest in improved network capability. If IT describes a need to reduce latency this will either not be understood or will mean little to non-IT staff. The business will happily participate, however, in a discussion of ways to improve the quality of conversations on IP phones.

IT Loves Jargon and Three Letter Acronyms

IT makes presentations, writes documentation and provides ongoing user help. Whenever the vocabulary used is not familiar to the audience, however, there is a barrier to understanding. Non-IT audiences can be confused when confronted by terms such as fiber-channel and blades. Even apparently common words, such as uploading, can be confusing for many people. While inappropriate use of jargon is not unique to IT, it is a major culprit. In a survey of general managers, 42% identified IT as the worst culprit, with sales and lawyers in second and third place with 20% and 16% respectively.

Reduce the Jargon

The use of jargon has at least three negative outcomes:

- **The audience stops listening** – When confused, people stop concentrating on subsequent messages. Proposals to management will not get the right attention, and may get rejected because the approvers don't understand. In training, staff will not learn what they are supposed to learn.
- **The audience may misunderstand but not admit to it** – Staff may be embarrassed to ask questions in training, and may then misuse or underuse equipment or software. Productivity opportunities will be lost and the help desk will have extra work.
- **The audience may become skeptical of the message** – Audiences often believe that those who use jargon are purposely confusing them to hide a problem or are pumping up the importance of the message. Credibility is lost and will be difficult to recover.

Consider the Audience and Their Knowledge About Technology

IT is always proud of its technology and its specifications. However, the audience typically has little interest or familiarity with the technology. They care about how the technology will affect the way things are done. Financial managers pay attention to cost and risk. Business managers listen to information on process change and improvement. Whenever a point of view is not relevant to the audience, even jargon-free material generates confusion.

For example, consider how IT should describe the projected installation of a new Storage Area Network. For the non IT audience, IT should communicate how the system will support business growth, will eliminate data losses and will cost less. The business does not care about iSCSI connections, RAID and the difference to direct-attached storage. Even an IT application group, while conversant with the technical terms, may be more interested in how the new storage system will allow quicker addition of storage capacity at peak periods.

Recommendations

1. **When communicating with non IT staff actively eliminate IT jargon.** They will listen more and hear better.
2. **Use tools to identify jargon in written material.** There are free tools that identify the amount of jargon within MSWord documents.
3. **When explaining ideas to a non IT audience, recognize what's important to them.**
   - Describe benefits in business not technical terms.
   - Quantify value.
   - Describe performance in business terms not technical terms.
4. **Improve IT staff understanding of the business perspective.**
   - Establish training programs.
   - Align analysts and maintenance staff with their customers.
   - Encourage business certification for IT staff.
5. **Reduce the use of jargon even within IT.** The IT community is diverse. Jargon, such as iSCSI or MPLS, which is familiar to a data center or infrastructure team, may not be familiar to an application team.

In Summary

IT professionals are comfortable with computer terminology; users of the technology are not. The use of unfamiliar jargon by IT can result in management rejecting good proposals or in staff losing productivity. Improve communication with the business by discussing IT in terms that are meaningful to them.

Cloud Computing

SOME OF THE BENEFITS:

- *Reduced Cost*
  Cloud technology is paid incrementally, saving organizations money.
- *Increased Storage*
  Organizations can store more data than on private computer systems.
- *Highly Automated*
  No longer do IT personnel need to worry about keeping software up to date.
- *Flexibility*
  Cloud computing offers much more flexibility than past computing methods.
- *More Mobility*
  Employees can access information wherever they are, rather than having to remain at their desks.
- *Allows IT to Shift Focus*
  No longer having to worry about constant server updates and other computing issues, organizations will be free to concentrate on innovation and running their core business.

WHY CLOUD COMPUTING?

Cloud computing has matured from a buzzword to a dynamic infrastructure used today by several organizations, yet many technology experts have differing views about what it means to the IT landscape and what cloud computing can do for business.

However, leading analysts including thought leaders from Gartner, Forrester, and IDC agree that this new model offers significant advantages for fast paced startups, SMBs and enterprises alike.

Cloud Application Characteristics:

Because cloud computing is related to a number of other technologies, it is best defined by the presence of a number of characteristics. These represent ideals that people want for the applications that run on the cloud:

- Incremental Scalability. Cloud environments allow users to access additional compute resources on-demand in response to increased application loads.
- Agility. As a shared resource, the cloud provides flexible, automated management to distribute the computing resources among the cloud's users.
- Reliability and Fault-Tolerance. Cloud environments take advantage of the built-in redundancy of the large numbers of servers that make them up by enabling high levels of availability and reliability for applications that can take advantage of this.
- Service-oriented. The cloud is a natural home for service-oriented applications, which need a way to easily scale as services get incorporated into other applications.
- Utility-based. Users only pay for the services they use, either by subscription or transaction-based models.
- Shared. By enabling IT resources to be consolidated, multiple users share a common infrastructure, allowing costs to be more effectively managed without sacrificing the security of each user's data.
- SLA-driven. Clouds are managed dynamically based on service-level agreements that define policies like delivery parameters, costs, and other factors.
- APIs. Because clouds *virtualize* resources as a service they must have an application programming interface (API).

Future of the Cloud

Industry analysts including Gartner and Forrester are early proponents of cloud computing and its potential. Several trends are emerging that will enable enterprises to make good use of cloud computing, such as shared, virtualized and automated IT architectures. However, the introduction of cloud enabled application platforms will certainly accelerate cloud adoption among businesses of all sizes.

In Summary

Cloud computing has many more benefits than negative attributes, cost reductions, better service levels, paying for only what you use, reducing over allocations. These and other factors make the cloud a good strategy for many organizations.

DISCLAIMER

The author and publisher have used their best efforts in preparing the information found in this book. The author and publisher make no representation or warranties with respect to the accuracy, applicability, fitness, or completeness of the contents of this book. The information contained in this book is strictly for educational purposes. Therefore, if you wish to apply ideas contained in this book, you are taking full responsibility for your actions.

EVERY EFFORT HAS BEEN MADE TO ACCURATELY REPRESENT THIS PRODUCT AND IT'S POTENTIAL. HOWEVER, THERE IS NO GUARANTEE THAT YOU WILL IMPROVE IN ANY WAY USING THE TECHNIQUES AND IDEAS IN THESE MATERIALS. EXAMPLES IN THESE MATERIALS ARE NOT TO BE INTERPRETED AS A PROMISE OR GUARANTEE OF ANYTHING. IMPROVEMENT POTENTIAL IS ENTIRELY DEPENDENT ON THE PERSON USING THIS PRODUCTS, IDEAS AND TECHNIQUES.

YOUR LEVEL OF IMPROVEMENT IN ATTAINING THE RESULTS CLAIMED IN OUR MATERIALS DEPENDS ON THE TIME YOU DEVOTE TO THE PROGRAM, IDEAS AND TECHNIQUES MENTIONED, KNOWLEDGE AND VARIOUS SKILLS. SINCE THESE FACTORS DIFFER ACCORDING TO INDIVIDUALS, WE CANNOT GUARANTEE YOUR SUCCESS OR IMPROVEMENT LEVEL. NOR ARE WE RESPONSIBLE FOR ANY OF YOUR ACTIONS.

MANY FACTORS WILL BE IMPORTANT IN DETERMINING YOUR ACTUAL RESULTS AND NO GUARANTEES ARE MADE THAT YOU WILL ACHIEVE RESULTS SIMILAR TO OURS OR ANYBODY ELSE'S, IN FACT NO GUARANTEES ARE MADE THAT YOU WILL ACHIEVE ANY RESULTS FROM OUR IDEAS AND TECHNIQUES IN OUR MATERIAL.

The author and publisher disclaim any warranties (express or implied), merchantability, or fitness for any particular purpose. The author and publisher shall in no event be held liable to any party for any direct, indirect, punitive, special, incidental or other consequential damages arising directly or indirectly from any use of this material, which is provided "as is", and without warranties.

As always, the advice of a competent professional should be sought.

The author and publisher do not warrant the performance, effectiveness or applicability of any sites listed or linked to in this report. All links are for information purposes only and are not warranted for content, accuracy or any other implied or explicit purpose.

www.ingramcontent.com/pod-product-compliance
Lightning Source LLC
Chambersburg PA
CBHW071423050326
40689CB00010B/1956